To Stacy

KICK⦿ASS
CORPORATE WIFE

Learn The Secrets Of A Woman Who Married Well & **Resurrected** *The Traditional Role In Marriage*

5 Steps To Creating A Foundation In Your Marriage

SUSAN BURLINGAME

Susan Burlingame

Kick-Ass Corporate Wife: Learn the Secrets of a Woman Who Married Well & Resurrected the Traditional Role in Marriage. 5 Steps to Creating a Foundation In Your Marriage

ISBN 978-0-9981804-1-0

Published by:
Susan Burlingame Enterprises, LLC.
7660 Fay Avenue H-360
La Jolla, California 92037
800-668-5948
www.SusanBurlingame.com

DISCLAIMER: I didn't include the names of some nice people to maintain their privacy. I also didn't include the names of some inelegant people as I'm no longer offended, or at least as annoyed as I used to be, and I don't want to embarrass them or their descendants. Or if I think someone might threaten to sue me or try to pick a fight.

I'd rather write than fight.

Although I am a self-proclaimed Kick-Ass Corporate Wife and advisor, reading this book does not create a reader-therapist relationship between us. This book should not be used as a substitute for the advice of a professional therapist or competent counselor admitted or authorized to practice in your jurisdiction.

Cover Photography by Monique Feil.
Makeup Styling by Antonella Annibale.
Illustrations by Anthony Woolf.

Dedication

This book is dedicated to my mother, Kathryn Ann—
the traditional Corporate Wife who puts the K-A in Kick-Ass!

Contents

Preface

What comes to mind when you read the words "Corporate Wife"?

Perhaps you envision—

- A woman who is bored, sadly waiting in the shadow of her husband's busy life

- A woman who numbs herself by shopping all day, buying whatever she wants

- A woman who has to entertain constantly, listening to and conversing with people

- A woman who is twenty to thirty years her husband's junior whose primary task is to maintain a pretty face and nice figure

Rarely has she been perceived as "kick-ass."

And, for the record, "kick-ass" is not a term I frequently use, or even feel totally comfortable with broadcasting to the world as the title of this book. But the term is relevant, applicable, and after getting my mother's approval—she assured me, "Your grandmother would have gotten a kick out of you using it"—I determined it was a much better title than *Kick-Donkey Corporate Wife*. My father even had the nickname "Kickie" when he was a child, for reasons unknown, so it seems I shouldn't fight the current with the title!

At the time of this writing, I am celebrating nine years of marriage to a busy, traveling, corporate executive. Although my story doesn't hold a candle to the Corporate Wife who has been happily married for decades, I have been indoctrinated quickly into this role, so I know what it takes. As a wife and as a woman who excels in this exciting and challenging role, I was inspired when my husband came home from work one day and said, "Sweetie, you are kicking ass!"

Those simple words of encouragement inspired the book you're reading right now: *Kick-Ass Corporate Wife*. I certainly have limitations in my role as a Corporate Wife that remind me I'll never be perfect, and there's always going to be room for improvement. For you, the amazing Corporate Wife who is reading these words, if you feel overwhelmed, lonely, bored, or uncertain regarding what to do with your day (or your life), I've been there and I get it!

But here's the deal. If you're going to be a Corporate Wife, you might as well be kick-ass about it. So, welcome! I'm really happy you're here. Let's continue on this journey together, and we can start right now!

Introduction

Dear Friend,

Welcome to *Kick-Ass Corporate Wife*.

I want to take a moment to share some thoughts with you about what to expect from this book.

This book assumes that you are equipped with some very basic tools—a working knowledge of what it means to be a Corporate Wife.

It also assumes—or hopes—that you come with a bit of gung-ho, an eagerness to become a better Corporate Wife because you recognize that it matters. I hope that you consider that there **IS more** to you than your "title" as a Corporate Wife—that you can **BECOME more** than your "title" as a Corporate Wife because you **ARE more** than a Corporate Wife. It also assumes—or hopes—that you've kicked to the curb the notion that only a select few, or those with unlimited funds, have what it takes to be a Kick-Ass Corporate Wife.

One—Participation Please!

First, this book is interactive. There are lots of opportunities for you to go deeper into the content, to download the accompanying workbook, and participate in my online blog community to learn of upcoming kick-ass events. You can also register to get updates to this book, as it gets expanded, at www.SusanBurlingame.com.

Two—Corporate Wives

Second, this book is written for Corporate Wives—women who are perceived as living in the shadows of their husbands' business success. The Corporate Wife (whose calling has been to be a wife, mother, stepmother, or homemaker) has a role that is distinct, and she has taken some flak over the years. There are millions of educated, intelligent, capable women who have taken on this supportive role, have made tremendous strides, and deserve some appreciation. Some of these women are already in the public eye, and some are just like you and me. Some may say that it is the husband who takes care of the Corporate Wife, but, in reality, she also takes care of him; it's a shared caretaking relationship with lots of work on both sides. This book is intended and written in the context of *mutual* honor and respect in marriage.

Three—All Wives

Third, this book is for all wives. You'll see there are LOTS of ideas that can be put into action in any marriage. Perhaps you don't consider yourself someone who "married well" (notice I didn't say "married rich"). Maybe you're reeling at the thought of staying in your marriage, wondering if the grass is greener elsewhere. I encourage you to stay where you are and learn to apply the principles of this book. If you're the type who's not looking for ways to do your role with excellence in your marriage, this book is not for you.

Four—The Curious

Fourth, this book is for anyone curious about the lives of Corporate Wives. It's designed to start a conversation with you, to give us a chance to get to know each other better, develop trust, a bond, and, ultimately, to decide if we should work together someday.

Five—The *What*

Fifth, this is a book that's packed with BIG content and lots of stories, ideas, and suggestions. It's both a WHAT book and a HOW-TO book. My intent for you, and the purpose of this book, is to show the most powerful ways to understand the particular step you are on in your role as a Corporate Wife and then to set you up for long-term success in your marriage. I have a how-to system available that includes everything you need in order to execute what you read in these pages.

Opportunities

You'll notice there are opportunities throughout this book to subscribe to my blog and register to receive some excellent free content. YES, I do have some great products I'd like to recommend and sell to you because they work and you'll have a better life with them. Regardless of the products, I offer lots of sage content to support you in your quest for a stronger marriage and more vibrant self.

If you don't like the book, that's okay. I'll refund your purchase. Just forward your Amazon receipt to my contact page at www.SusanBurlingame.com, and I will take care of you. Please don't leave a negative review because you found a spelling or grammatical error. Life's too short for complainers, okay? We can part as friends and just leave it at that.

Having said that, if you like what you read, or most of what you read, I'd absolutely, positively love to hear from you, get to know you better, and find out what you learned—or, better yet, post a picture through my social media channels at www.SusanBurlingame.com.

Five Steps

I've developed a 5-step system to determine which step and location you're on as a Kick-Ass Corporate Wife. With each step, I've included a corresponding *Action Plan* to help you put that step into effect immediately. Because, after all, you don't just want to read about it—you want to get moving on it.

To provide even more support, you'll find that I've included many places in this book called *Pause and Consider* where I ask you to reflect on your personal values, beliefs, hopes, dreams, and goals—all for the sake of giving you the time and space to develop greater clarity in your pursuit of becoming more.

As you read through this book and determine that you are a Kick-Ass Corporate Wife and have something to add, perhaps I could learn a thing or two from you, too! We're in this together, Corporate Wives. If you're feeling like you're not yet Kick-Ass, well . . . keep reading. You will be! You're on your way to being a Kick-Ass Corporate Wife.

The BEST way to start a relationship with me beyond this book is to visit www.SusanBurlingame.com, and post your comments on the comment wall. I'll see it and do my best to respond to you.

I'm looking forward to getting to know you better!

Sincerely,

Susan Burlingame

Susan Burlingame in San Diego, California, USA

1—Finding Common Ground

I always found that beauty and confidence are synonymous.
If you feel confident, that's what people see.
—Cindy Crawford, Model and Businesswoman

What did you just say?

I heard what I *think* you said, but I want to make sure I'm hearing you correctly.

Did you just say, "I can't relate to the Corporate Wife thing . . ."?

Okay, I hear you, but now I want to make sure you can hear me.

Who says you can't?!

What *is* a Corporate Wife? What does that title mean, really? What is the definition? And what does it mean to be a *Kick-Ass* Corporate Wife?

Please Introduce Yourself

When you're at a party, and someone you've never met comes up to you and says, "Tell me about you," where do you start?

If you're like most people, you start with "My name is _____, and I'm a _____."

Do you respond with a compelling title that reflects your identity?

If you answered no, don't fret. It's perfectly normal to fumble through an introduction with a stranger. In these situations, it's always helpful to have some kind of elevator pitch to pull out at a moment's notice. But don't worry about where this conversation is going because this is not a business book.

Getting Beyond the Introduction

Let's go deep for a moment, and discuss your foundation.

Is there anything missing that is causing you to not fill in the blank? What's missing from your title? What's missing from your relationship? What do you want and who do you want to be? Who do you want to become?

You have a title, but you just don't realize it. I'm sharing my title with you so that we can break down this barrier I've crowned myself with, and then we can relate to each other.

Let's break down three words, one at a time, and reverse them.

Why? Because . . . [*gasp!*] . . . you might be shocked to learn that the person sitting in your chair has a limited mindset. Yes, that means YOU. And yep, that means ME, too.

We *ALL* suffer from a limited mindset from time to time. It happens when we don't *believe*.

Breaking Down That Wall

My goal is to break down the barriers of our mindsets that limit our ability to relate to ourselves and to each other.

Let's break down the definitions of some keywords so that we can *believe* that we can inspire and encourage each other to have the courage to become more than we *think* we are.

By breaking down this title, we can realize the unlimited potential and possibilities of our lives, in doing what we are called to do. From there, we can go above and beyond what we can ask, think, or imagine for ourselves.

Our limiting beliefs are lies. They are not the truth. They are not real. And, dang it, our limited beliefs are in the way!

So, let's get real and get them out of our path.

The Simple Test

Let's get real with a simple 4-question test.

Ready, class? Get out your number 2 pencil. Here goes:

1 **Do you relate, in your role, to this definition of the word WIFE?**

   The definition of "wife":

   1 A married woman considered in relation to her spouse.

   2 The wife of a person with a specified occupation.

   3 A spouse, partner, life partner, mate, helpmate, bride.

   Based on this definition, are you a *wife*? Yes or No. Check the box:

   ❑ YES

   ❑ NO

2   **Does your husband relate, in his role, to this definition of the word CORPORATE?**

The definition of "corporate":

1   Of or relating to a corporation, especially a large company or group.

2   A united group of persons.

Based on this definition, is your husband working in a *corporate* capacity? Yes or No. Check the box:

❑ YES

❑ NO

3   **Does your role require you to be an EXTENSION of your husband's role as a professional?**

The definition of "extension":

1   A part that is added to something to prolong it. A continuation.

2   Enlarging the scope of something.

Based on this definition, are you an *extension* of your husband's corporate role? Yes or No. Check the box:

❑ YES

❑ NO

4 **Do you relate, in yourself, to this definition of the word KICK-ASS?**

The definition of "kick-ass":

1 Really cool, awesome, extremely good, impressive, excellent.

2 Sweet, amazing, hot, sexy, fun.

Based on this definition, are you "kick-ass"? Yes or No. Check the box:

❑ RESOUNDING YES

❑ NOT YET

If you answered yes to *at least* questions 1 and 2 of this test, then you and I have a foundation on which we can relate. We now have a starting point, you and I.

If you didn't answer yes to one or two of these questions, you and I have a starting point that you will, hopefully, agree to pursue further with an open mind and apply the principles of this book to your unique situation. If not, well, heck . . . we can agree to disagree.

Shining Some Light

In defining the title of this book, my goal is to shine some light on the starting point on that path that leads you on a journey through the context of the book's overall message. You and I have started our relationship with a conversation that creates our foundation. Together, we can become friends and partners, willingly, on this journey.

Get ready to think—to *pause and consider* what you questioned in the beginning and ask yourself: *Can I relate to this Corporate Wife thing?* Yes, it's somewhat intangible—I get it.

Ahem!

Please give me your full attention for just a moment. We're so busy these days we can't even *pause and consider* something. We're so distracted. It's hard to believe, but we don't even take the time to use our imaginations anymore.

When was the last time you took a moment to just get creative and free your mind?

We look up, and we see a ceiling instead of the sky. We don't even realize how limiting the voices are in our head. We don't even comprehend the power of listening to our own words when we say, "I can't imagine that . . ."

We listen to our *BUTs* when we say, "I want what she's got . . . BUT I can't imagine that."

Listen to me when I tell you, "Friend, that conversation needs to stop. You CAN imagine that!"

Years ago, I watched supermodel Cindy Crawford being interviewed. Cindy Crawford is married to Rande Gerber, an American entertainment industry businessman. Cindy is a successful American supermodel, international celebrity, and spokesperson. She once said something profound that has stuck with me through the years. I can't even find her quoted as saying it, but when I first heard her say it, I wrote it down. She said, "I hope that by seeing something beautiful in me, women will see something beautiful in themselves."

I *paused and considered* that statement, and it caused me to listen to what she said.

I *paused and considered* if I could imagine that.

I *paused and considered*—and responded, "YES! I can imagine that!"

I want what she's got! Granted, I don't want, or have what it takes, to be Cindy Crawford. She is uniquely Cindy Crawford. Her beauty is something I choose to celebrate. As I look deeper, peeling back the outer layer of her comment, in sharing her synonymous foundation of beauty and confidence, Cindy Crawford shared something that all of us can have: HOPE.

In the context of being a married woman with unique gifts, talents, and abilities, I am paying it forward by taking action with the same message. I hope that by seeing something beautiful in me, women will see something beautiful in themselves.

The Real Question

The real question to ask yourself is "What do I want?" or "What's missing?"

From this point on, as you read this book, here's what I want you to do:

Pause . . . and consider your marriage.

Pause . . . and consider your role and your husband's role in your marriage.

Pause . . . and consider yourself.

Pause . . . and consider all of your unlimited possibilities.

I am ready to take you with me. Are you ready? Good. Let's crank!

2—Let's Get Real Please, [House-] Wives!

Success for me is finding the courage to live your truest and biggest life.
—Sara Blakely, Businesswoman and Founder of Spanx

I can't hold it in any longer. "It" meaning—my humble opinion. I don't think *The Real Housewives of Orange County* is a bad television show. I actually think it's a pretty good show, and here's why: the show provides a temporary guilty pleasure of tantalizing entertainment to countless women around the world. It's a vortex of drama, pop-culture, and lifestyle entertainment all in one. It's the modern-day soap opera, resurrecting dramatic stories of the past, like *As the World Turns* and *Peyton Place*. We watched our mothers get distracted by these soap operas. Now we do too.

A little reality TV never hurt anyone, right?

The problem with a show, such as *The Real Housewives of Orange County*, is that it isn't just a "little reality TV" for many women who watch it. While viewers like you and me know where to draw the line between fantasy and reality, for some viewers, there is no line to this "reality." This "distraction" ends up creating a fantasy life that perpetuates an entitlement mentality in some households. I might sound a little far-fetched in saying so, but I've seen it happen.

This reality show exacerbates the perception that it's normal and perfectly acceptable to be a flippin' crazy housewife. Many of the characters behave badly, brawl with other women in public, degrade and humiliate their husbands (and ex-husbands), declare financial and moral bankruptcy, and (in another spin-off of the show) even go to prison to end up with a book deal to live happily ever after. Holy moly.

Why do these "real" women behave as they do? What is their motive? Is it all in the name of fame, fortune, and fantasy?

Climbing That Slippery Slope

Call me a Pollyanna if you will, but, dagnabbit, I have to limit that kind of negative influence on my life, my marriage, and my personal goals and dreams. Don't get me wrong, I'm all for a harmless, voyeuristic spin of life behind a prestigious gate and occasionally dumbing down for the sake of easing my mind. BUT it's a slippery slope.

Where's the foundation in the marriage? Where's the fatigue of true grit and sweat equity in the journey that results in getting to the other side?

I guess that's entertainment . . . but it's not anything that serves wives who want to create a foundation for excellence in, and beyond, marriage.

As someone who had a dream to be married, and is now married, I would like to watch a show that provides me with a modern-day *Housewife* role model. I would like to watch someone who helps me learn how to fulfill my own dreams instead of being a passive spectator, indulging in the celebrity of someone else's *reality* dream life.

Stay with me as I play the party pooper who disrupts your television time. Let's mute the TV for a moment while I ask you the same questions I'm asking myself.

Aren't there any women out there *who have an interest in watching and learning* from other *real* kick-ass women who function as highly evolved people within the context of solid marriages? Aren't there *real* kick-ass women in today's modern world who want to improve themselves and become more?

I'm betting that there are more than a few of us out there, and that's why I'm writing this book—so that you can have a navigational beacon for your path.

Whenever I learn the story of a real kick-ass woman who functions as a highly evolved person in the context of a successful marriage, I want to know her secrets and determine if there's something I want to listen to and incorporate into my own life.

A Real Kick-Ass Woman

Sara Blakely is the founder of Spanx and the youngest female self-made billionaire. Sara is married to Jesse Itzler, the vice chairman of Marquis Jet Partners, Inc., one of the largest private jet companies in the world. Sara is, by my definition, a Corporate Wife, and I believe that she's a Kick-Ass Corporate Wife too.

In an interview with Darren Hardy in *Success Magazine*, she said that when she was growing up, her father would encourage her and her siblings to fail each week. If they weren't failing enough and trying enough new things, her father would be disappointed. This "failing" philosophy is something I am learning to apply to my life. If "failing" worked for Sara Blakely, how can it work for me? We are so afraid to fail, yet she has proved that failing propelled her forward.

Sarah Blakely is a great example of someone who had the courage to fail so that she could live her truest and biggest life. Her journey that landed her in the coveted role as a successful businessperson and Corporate Wife didn't happen overnight—it started in her childhood. One step at a time—failing. Her story is real. I don't compare Sara to one of the "Real Housewives." Do you?

As a woman who married well and stepped into a coveted role as a Corporate Wife in Southern California, I guess, in that sense, you could compare me to one of the "Real Housewives." I don't necessarily look like one, or maybe I do? Maybe I seem like one in person to those who don't know me and are fooled by the "rocks that I got."

But if you judge me by my plain wedding band, which I wear the majority of the time, chances are you're not going to find me flipping tables in a restaurant or throwing a glass of wine in my girlfriend's face. Thankfully, I have a solid foundation. *I'm still Susie from the Midwest.*

Pause and Consider

As one Corporate Wife to another, I'm sure you've also been compared to one of the "Real Housewives" or else you've been perceived, perhaps negatively, differently than how you really are.

- In what ways do you fit these perceptions?

- In what ways do you differ?

- How do you handle it when others put these stereotypes on you?

Just Doin' My Job

Early on, after having stepped into my role as a Corporate Wife, I hadn't given my "job" much consideration in regard to the perspective of the jury of my peers. When I went to my first high school reunion, having skipped the first two, one of my former, smarty-pants classmates saw me and hugged me with surprise, declaring, "Oh, I thought you were someone's trophy wife!" I stepped back with a dumbfounded look on my face, thinking, "What is THAT supposed to mean . . . ?!"

Meanwhile, my husband Kevin, who takes personal pride in these situations, with his eyes looking sideways at me, nodded his head up and down and mouthed, "Oh, HECK yeah!" He loved it! Go figure.

Definition of *trophy wife*: an informal term for a wife, usually young and attractive, who is regarded as a status symbol for the husband, who is often an older and wealthy "sugar daddy."

Now that I look back on my classmate's comment, I'm so grateful that I became someone unrecognizable from my former self. Doesn't everyone want to be seen as a better version of themselves as the years go by? I'm so grateful for her insightful words. If not for her comment, I may not have made the foundation to start this conversation with you.

Judging My Cover

Like it or not, the truth is—we all, so to speak, judge a book by its cover. Her comment was compelling to me. Her comment propelled me forward to dig deeper into how this trophy wife perception limits women. There's a distinction between a trophy wife in the true sense of the word "trophy" and caring about your appearance.

Here's the reality: I am doing my darndest to be the latter and NOT to become a frumpy wife. I am not going down without a fight. When it comes to the inevitable downward gravitational pull that comes with age—wrinkles, cellulite, varicose veins, raging hormones—everything that makes me want to say *UGH* . . . I'm puttin' up my dukes for as long as I can. If someone mistakes me for a trophy wife in the process, I must be doing something right in my gravity fight. I'll take it!

My point is this—as a Corporate Wife, living a blessed Southern California life, there's an unspoken code that you keep your looks up. This code actually creates mutual benefits for you and for your husband. Why wouldn't I want to do all I can to be healthy, to do my best to look and feel great? I've heard another wife agree with me, explaining it this way, "It's our JOB to be beautiful."

Unspoken code or not, job or not, I'm someone who strives to do my best to look good for myself AND remain attractive to my husband. I also want to do my best to fulfill my role in the best way possible for myself AND for my husband. There's something inside me that doesn't seek perfection, but aims for excellence. It's the way I choose to present myself to the world.

The *Other-Centered* Approach

My views may seem old-fashioned, but I prefer to look at them as a resurrection of the traditional in this modern day. My parents recently celebrated 65 years of marriage in traditional roles. My father, now retired, fulfilled his role in business as the financial provider. My mother continues to fulfill her role as his supportive wife. Based on the odds set against them when they eloped at a young age, they defied the precedents about what was required from the start to have a successful, long-lasting, loving marriage.

From my parents and their marriage, I then ask myself, "What can I do to resurrect their marital success in the modern world we live in? How can I be the outlier Corporate Wife who defies the dismal marital statistics?"

I am shining the light at the beginning of the path. The pathway starts by taking a cue from my parents and creating a foundation for our relationship. My husband and I together are "other-centered" as a team, meaning we make a concentrated effort to be focused on each other's needs (versus each's own needs). As best we can, we aim to present ourselves to the world in a humble manner.

I'm reminded of the times my dad would tell me about Tom Osborn, the respected past coach of the Nebraska football team. My dad said Tom Osborn always encouraged his football players to simply make the touchdown and get back in the game. There was no happy dance or moonwalk to celebrate what a player was expected to do—it was his job. That's different than today.

I'm all for celebrating a job well done, but where's the humility? It's about "the touchdown" and not about the job. What happened to just doing your job in humble service?

Kevin and I simply do our best to lead fairly quiet lives, in the midst of a fast-paced lifestyle, while staying actively engaged and present with each other in the modern world we live in. We continually feed our marriage to keep it happy. What started before the honeymoon phase—as a seed—in our relationship continues to grow and simply happens because we love and care about each other. We choose to cultivate a wonderful life together. Why? Because we're grateful for each other and for what we have. We've been entrusted with amazing blessings. We want peace and tranquility in our home. We want to do our individual jobs well. We want our marriage to grow, flourish, and build upon the dream we shared when we both said, "I do."

What's the alternative?

Pause and Consider

- In what ways do you and your spouse practice the "other-centered" approach?

- Where is this approach lacking in your relationship, on your part and on his?

- If this approach is seriously lacking, what can you do about it?

That Grass Over There . . .

Well, friend, you and I both know the grass on the other side is NOT greener. You probably have, and I certainly have, seen the results of spouses who have experienced the pain and agony of the end of a dream, the loss experienced from betrayal in a marriage where one or both partners were not actively engaged, present, and happy.

I have witnessed the sad truth that there are spouses out there who watch the so-called "entertainment" of *reality* television and live vicariously through the television characters. The shows are entertaining, yet subtly enticing and crafty as they create a twisting of the truth that can send spouses down a path that gets off course, sometimes in an instant.

I've witnessed the Tasmanian devil cloud of dust that is left in the path of these blankety-blank spouses—male or female—who wreak destruction on their own marriages. I've witnessed marriages that crumble due to narcissism, entitlement philosophies, and clinically diagnosed personality disorders. The out-of-touch-with-reality spouse is not self-aware, and is too focused on "what I get" versus "all that I lose." For the spouse left in the dust, it eventually becomes a worthless effort to waste their own breath to find resolutions. The marriage crumbles.

Here's the really sad part: not only does the marriage take a sucker punch, but everyone associated with the marriage suffers too. A marriage that fizzles takes a huge toll on more than the couple divorcing. It affects immediate and extended family members. If the marriage doesn't end early, before kids are involved, it disrupts the lives and dreams of innocent children. It divides and ruins mutual friendships. It takes a devastating financial toll on everyone involved, and the one who set out in greed rarely ends up with the big payoff. When the gravy train eventually stops, they get to experience what it feels like to choke on the dust of their own regret.

So who really benefits?

The lawyers . . . why, I oughta . . . [*shake fist!*]

Pause and Consider

- Take a moment and recall couples you know that indulged in the "grass is greener over there" that likely led to crumbling marriages and vicious divorces.

- Explore within your own psyche what factors have ever tempted you to look at the neighbor's lawn.

- I'm assuming you are reading this book because you are already committed and want to take it to the next level from good to better to kick-ass best. Record that commitment in your journal.

So, just in case you're wondering, my friend, why I bring this up, it's because it is one of the real and raw reasons I wrote this book—I want to start the conversation that gets real about the life of the woman who marries well and steps into the role of a Corporate Wife. I want to shed some light on the truth and expand that premise farther that there are women, like you and me, who recognize all that we have, appreciate it, feel grateful for it, and desire to take action and do something more with it: to live our truest and biggest lives while keeping our marriages intact.

Women like us have focus, and we have a goal—to be a lot *more* kick-ass in our Corporate Wife role.

So how do we get there, and where do we start?

You took the first step with your initiative. Just your having picked up this book and read this far shows me that you are compelled by the premise of this conversation. It is my guess that you continually seek to have the marriage of your dreams, and you are willing to work on yourself to be the woman you've always dreamed of becoming—all within the context of your happy marriage. To me, that says you're kick-ass! You may not always feel like you're kick-ass, but guess what? I just said you were!

And ta-da . . . that makes it so. Stick with me, and I'll show you how you will not only learn to believe it, but you will see it AND really believe it! Let me empower you with confidence because you've got what it takes.

Your Journey

Not to toot my own horn, but to kinda toot my own horn, I am living proof that you can crack the code and find purpose and fulfillment within the context of your happy marriage. I believe, and many of my friends are witness to it, that I am living the life of my dreams.

Is my life perfect? Oh, HECK, no. Living a perfect life isn't my dream, and perfect doesn't mean happy.

Is my life all about money? No. I don't love money. I love what money can do. Money can give freedom and peace of mind. But money doesn't do a lot of things. Money definitely doesn't buy happiness. I've learned that having more money often creates bigger problems.

Is my life complete because I'm married? No. I don't believe marriage guarantees happiness. It was my dream to be married, and I love being married, but marriage itself doesn't make me complete or happy.

Happiness, in my humble opinion, comes from fulfilling your life's calling, the calling that provides you with a sense of purpose. In this book, I am sharing how, as a Corporate Wife, I find fulfillment by taking my sense of purpose to a higher level.

If your vision is to take your Corporate Wife role to the highest level—that of Kick-Ass Corporate Wife—then I will help you move forward.

In order to move forward, the FIRST STEP is to have VISION.

What is your vision for your marriage?

My vision for my marriage is to have a relationship where both of us are "other-centered." This vision may sound small, but it's actually quite immense for two people to be centered on the other. It takes work. This vision created our foundation and became the underlying principle for the way we are creating our dream life together as a married couple.

What does it mean to have VISION?

Having vision can mean a lot of things to different people, but to me it's like wanting to be in that place that stops time. It's the BIG picture. It's like imagining a wonderful dream. It's like waving a magic wand. It's like a big, blank canvas on which to paint a picture of your own design. It's like a blank check tied to a bank account with unlimited funds. Vision is abundance at its core.

While you should know that you are already equipped with everything you need to live a productive and full life—as you are intended—this vision inside you still isn't going to do you, or anyone else, any good if it doesn't get out of you. You have to tap into it. You have to believe, without a shadow of a doubt, that you have what it takes to express your confidence in your vision with an overflowing mindset.

STEP 1, in my five-step approach to being a Kick-Ass Corporate Wife, is VISION. You've got to articulate and then actualize your VISION.

And here's the interesting news—my approach is continually evolving. You will repeatedly have opportunities to grow, to begin again with a new vision, and to learn how to keep evolving as a person. You will not ever stagnate in your life with my approach. You will not be left disappointed by the process.

Here's what I suggest you do. Keep reading. Keep thinking of yourself during the time that you read this book. Personalize the rest of these chapters, and make them your own. Follow each *Action Plan* as you go. When you come across, a *Pause and Consider*, take a moment to really do it. You, your life, your dreams, and your marriage are worth it!

This isn't a race. There's no "test" that you must pass. This book won't give you that recurring nightmare of a flunked college exam. (Holy schnikeys, I hate waking up after that one!) This book is here to help you succeed with an A+ at every stage.

Your assignment from here on out is to read each chapter and during the chapters, take the time to *Pause and Consider*. I highly recommend that you download the companion encouragement guide to give you even more support in responding to the *Pause and Consider* questions. By writing out your responses, you will engage more deeply with the questions and establish a record in time of where you stand. You can revisit your responses over the coming weeks, months, and years to see how you've stayed true to your big life vision and also to see how you've grown and achieved your dreams. Don't be afraid to write down your vision, dreams, and goals—it's how they get accomplished!

You'll also find at the end of several chapters, a simple *Action Plan* that will guide you in putting the chapter's recommendation into effect immediately.

That's it! Easy-peasy, right?

There's no need to rush, but momentum is your friend.

Use this time to think, reflect, and dream about the things that are completely YOU.

The rest of this story is about YOU, discovering your unique abilities and how YOU can make your mark on the world while being a Kick-Ass Corporate Wife.

No pressure, right?

Right—you got this!

Am I ever excited to be on the bus with you! Get out of the passenger seat, 'cuz I'm ready for YOU to be in the driver's seat.

Big Chapter Takeaways

- When the Corporate Wife does something for her husband or to fulfill her Corporate Wife role, she is, in effect, also doing it for herself.

- The Corporate Wife doesn't play out the drama she sees on reality TV shows or in the desperate, dramatic, and sad lives of other couples. She strives to have an honorable and respectful marriage.

- STEP 1 is VISION. The Corporate Wife has VISION to create a solid foundation for her marriage. She aims for a relationship of abundance, a relationship in which she and her husband operate as an "other-centered" team, with each spouse taking into account the other's needs. It is through your VISION that you resurrect your traditional role in marriage. It is the first step.

Up Next

In order for you to gain greater perspective on your marriage and your role as a Corporate Wife, I'm going to share with you some of my personal history. In the next chapter, you'll learn how I came to realize that there are perceptions of the Corporate Wife role that are not completely true. You will learn how I chose to disrupt these perceptions and how I developed my vision for the new Corporate Wife reality: an earned position of responsibility, respect, and honor.

First Action Plan

Download the Kick-Ass Corporate Wife Encouragement Guide that you can use as your sacred place to engage with the *Pause and Consider* questions in this book. Make sure to review these from the first chapter and actually record your responses in your journal.

You can download the companion workbook, Kick-Ass Corporate Wife Encouragement Guide, at **www.SusanBurlingame.com/Book1**

Establish a particular time and place in your day for the next few weeks that you will dedicate to slowly reading this book and carefully working through the personal development, soul-searching activities we'll be doing together.

Yes, it takes some planning, time, and energy to be kick-ass, but you've got what it takes. Plus, we're in this together!

3—An Abundance Perspective

*I have learned to replace a lot of talk with an alternative talk
that has gotten me through more doors than anything else.
You know what? I have a right to be here!*
—Barbara Corcoran, Businesswoman and TV Personality
on ABC's Shark Tank

Two months ago, I ran into my neighbor as I was walking out the door of our beach house. I usually stay at our beach house for a few days at a time, so she inquired about the length of my stay. I shared that my husband was entertaining clients on a sport fishing expedition for the next couple of days and that I would be in town until it was over.

Then she asked how I felt about my frequently changing schedule and my constant back-and-forth between homes in a way that suggested she was fishing for a potential issue. I simply, yet honestly, replied, "I love it!" I wasn't completely sure that she believed me, so I elaborated, "My role suits me well. I believe that all along I have been preparing for our busy schedule and for our lifestyle. It does require some juggling and keeping on top of things, but it keeps me organized."

Instead of pressing further, she switched gears toward being more complimentary, declaring, "You both seem so happy and well-suited for each other. You're always going out and doing fun things together, or going to interesting places." And then she surprised me by adding, "I wish I could have your life . . . for just one week. I'd love to experience it."

This comment brings us to a frequently encountered theme—the *perception* of the life of the Corporate Wife. Does she have a life that is fancied by other people? Is her life considered somewhat mysterious? This isn't the first time I've heard someone tell me that they wished they could have my life. I've heard it from other women. Heck, I've even heard it from men!

All Your Wishes Granted

The winter after Kevin and I got married, we were enjoying an evening with a group of friends who were hanging out at our cabin in the Sierra Mountains for a ski vacation. We were playing a game called "Table Topics" in the downstairs bar area. This game is a fun conversation starter that gets people talking with a card that asks a thought-provoking question. When one guy in the group was asked, "What would your life be like if you had all of your wishes granted?" without missing a beat, he turned and pointed to me, declaring, "My life would be like Susan's!"

Everyone agreed and laughed out loud, myself included. But after a few moments of consideration, they realized that the answer wasn't really true. No one really wanted my life because they knew that the perception of it was not exactly the reality. They knew what was involved in my day-to-day, and although the perception sounded dreamy, the reality of it was something that, on second thought, wasn't quite reflective of living out the genie-in-a-bottle scenario.

Pause and Consider

- Recall some instances when others have pushed their perceptions of the Corporate Wife Life onto you. (Yes, we've already hit upon this issue, but because it is so prevalent, let's address it again!)

- How did those perceptions jive with your reality? If other people think your life is to be envied, do you agree?

- How did you handle those interactions— were there times you were miffed and you showed it? Were there times you bit your tongue and played oblivious? Have you ever bothered to explore the truth with anyone in an honest and non-disparaging way? If so, how did it play out?

STUDS and STARS—No Thank You

Back in the 1980s, there was a term that was coined for the wife of a traveling executive who was temporarily or permanently residing in a country other than that of their citizenship, also known as an expatriate or expat. At the time, the term was "trailing spouse." Most expat spouses of today take offense at that term because it is antiquated and derogatory.

Today, other euphemisms exist, "accompanying spouse" or "accompanying partner." There are even more politically correct acronyms, such as "STUDS" ([male] spouses trailing under duress successfully) or "STARS" (spouses traveling and relocating successfully). In the end, none of these terms resonates with me or reflects the modern wife of today's executive whom I have come to know and frequently meet.

I believe the time has come for these women to have a term that adequately reflects what their important position implies—a position of respect and honor, a position that is essential and completely transcending of any derogatory role comparison, such as one implying that a supportive spouse is merely an extra piece of baggage or an appendage.

So, in consideration of an appropriate term, I was reminded of something that was said to me back in my career-girl days. I had a sales manager who would ask our sales team what we did to "earn your seat" as a salesperson in the office. Applying this principle to the modern-day relationship of the Corporate Wife and her corporate husband, I believe "earning your seat" is a two-way street! For this reason, I decided to take the term Corporate Wife and coin it, "Kick-Ass Corporate Wife."

Barbara Corcoran, American businesswoman, investor, speaker, consultant, syndicated columnist, author, and television personality on ABC's *Shark Tank*, is a great example of a woman who earned her seat. Barbara is married to her second husband, Bill Higgins. In an interview with Darren Hardy of *Success Magazine*, she talked about her philosophy during her early days as a waitress, wanting to be her own boss and co-founding a real estate business. She had the "earn your seat" mindset: "No one can tell me I'm not welcome here. I have the right to be as successful and as rich as I want, and I'm working my buns off. I have to get myself going like that OFTEN just to get through a door I need to go through. Once you go through that door, you're smarter than you think you are." Barbara is living proof that it starts with taking a step through that door.

Whatever your dream, even if it's not to compete in the business world, you can believe that you are qualified to compete in any race. And it all starts with that initial step through the door.

She's NOT . . .

So, let me explain what the Kick-Ass Corporate Wife is *not*. She is not lacking strength, brains, or creativity. She's not someone who is in her role because she's excluded from the workforce. As I said earlier, she's not to be confused with the stereotypical "trophy" wife or the "real" housewife of many cities. She's not a homemaker who does nothing. She's not in her role for the money.

She Is . . .

Now that you know what the Kick-Ass Corporate Wife is *not*, let me tell you more about what she *is*. She is encouraging. She is loving. She is strong. She is wise, and she is a contributor.

The reality of her life is that she starts out on her journey, as many wives do, learning the basics of the role of a supportive spouse. This learning curve can be short or long, but she doesn't learn the basics overnight. It involves creating a foundation for her marriage, and a vision for her relationship with her husband.

So—what's your VISION for yourself as the wife of that busy guy who's got his nose in his job?

In order to move forward from your VISION, you must take a STEP forward.

STEP 2, in my five-step approach to being a Kick-Ass Corporate Wife, is to take a STEP toward your marital VISION.

You must move forward with a STEP—a specific action—toward determining, creating, and paying attention to the sensibilities of who you are and what you love. You then establish the foundation for the future life you will love even more as each day moves forward. Moving forward, going forward.

The important thing to remember after creating your VISION to be a Kick-Ass Corporate Wife is this: you start by taking a

STEP. It is the place where you take your resurrected, traditional role in marriage and reinvent it for yourself.

The role of the Corporate Wife has distinct differences from the traditional wife role due to the unique responsibilities required that are closely connected with her husband's career. I'll be elaborating on these unique responsibilities later in this book.

 Pause and Consider

- In what ways do you agree or disagree with my "She's NOT . . ." and "She Is . . ." assessments of the Corporate Wife?

- What can you add on to the "She's NOT . . ." and "She Is . . ." assessments?

Big Chapter Takeaways

- There are lots of (mis-)perceptions out there about what it means to live the Corporate Wife Life, so the Corporate Wife needs to prepare herself for hearing them and reacting to them with dignity and grace.

- While there are lots of derogatory titles for the Corporate Wife, i.e., trailing spouse and trophy wife, the title we prefer is "Kick-Ass Corporate Wife."

- The Corporate Wife should never give in to the negative perceptions concerning her role. Instead, she should feel grounded in knowing all that she is and does—which as we know, is a lot. She can also feel great about living an abundant life.

- STEP 2 is a STEP FORWARD. The Corporate Wife with a VISION for her marriage takes a STEP FORWARD toward that vision. It is through the STEP FORWARD that you take action to resurrect your vision and move your vision forward toward the desired abundant marriage.

Up Next

As we move forward, I will be sharing my "10 Secrets" to success through stories that share my transformation from normal to Kick-Ass Corporate Wife. As you read, you may find that your experience differs greatly from mine or your results aren't the same, so I ask you to stay with me and share your experiences in the Comments section of my blog posts, or on my Contact page at **www.SusanBurlingame.com**; that way we can create a conversation among Corporate Wives, and learn from each other.

As I said before, I'm taking a risk calling myself a Kick-Ass Corporate Wife because I could be perceived as tooting my own horn. But in the end, I hope you will see *yourself* as a Kick-Ass Corporate Wife through my stories, and, if you haven't done so already, apply some of these upcoming "secrets" to finding purpose and fulfillment in your life to further enhance your marriage as a Kick-Ass Corporate Wife.

Second Action Plan

Prepare a standard response that is both graceful and informatory that you can deliver at a moment's notice when you get hit with one of these not-so-pleasant Corporate Wife stereotypes. Please share it in our Corporate Wife community forum, especially about how it played out when you actually applied it in real life.

4—What's Behind Your Counter?

So many women just don't know how great they really are. They come to us all vogue on the outside and vague on the inside.
—Mary Kay Ash, Businesswoman and Founder
of Mary Kay Cosmetics, Inc.

What's Her Secret?

We've covered the *perception* of the life of the Corporate Wife—that it's a fancied life to behold. We've also covered the underlying message of the *real* and (implied) *desperate* housewife. Whether stuck in a house or within her own mind, any woman might feel bound, confined, and disempowered. Feelings such as these are *not* an indication that the only option is to give in to temptation, or entitlement, and wander over to the dark side of the *real* and the *desperate*.

So, let's take a deep breath, put our shoulders back, and put a new frame on the picture. It's time to take a posture check and discover the answer to the question that the neighbors are fishing for . . .

What's *really* going on behind the scenes?

Let's move on to what really matters—the *reality* of the life of the Kick-Ass Corporate Wife, which I'm sharing with you in the form of *secrets*. You'll notice that these *secrets* don't eliminate people's perceptions of the Corporate Wife (so as not to *ruin* the allure and mystique) but instead *reveal* (as I will describe later in the book) the truth as to what enables the Corporate Wife to be Kick-Ass—because she has *more behind the counter than what is on display.*

10 Secrets to Being Vogue on the Inside

Marriage takes work. The added element of being a Corporate Wife creates additional work because of the demands placed on you in regard to your responsibilities, your connections to your husband's business, your lifestyle, and the choices that are made in your marriage. There's a lot going on behind the scenes for the Corporate Wife that many people don't realize. What is on display for the neighbors to see doesn't reflect the glacier of challenges that often lies deep beneath the surface.

The challenges a Corporate Wife experiences are not always on display, and that's a good thing. You may often *feel* like you're constantly juggling, or being tested with the demands this role requires, but others *think* you're not juggling because you're handling your responsibilities as if your corporate marriage is a successful business. In other words, it runs like a well-oiled machine. Regardless, no matter who you are, you can't always be prepared for the most difficult challenges that come your way. In those moments, you must learn to think on your feet, improvise, and keep moving forward regardless of the juggling or the magnitude of the tests. This is nothing new, for Corporate Wives have experienced such challenges for generations.

An excellent role model and example for us is the late Mary Kay Ash, one of America's most respected businesswomen. Decades ago, she experienced such modern-day challenges as divorce and one of the worst of challenges—the death of her spouse— yet she managed to persevere with strength and improvisation to fulfill her vision.

Mary Kay Ash, the widely respected American businesswoman and founder of Mary Kay Cosmetics, Inc., advocated "praising people to success." She was married to her first husband, Ben Rogers, at the age of 17. While her husband served in World War II, she sold books door-to-door. After her husband's return, they divorced. She wrote a book to assist women in business, and when the book turned into a business plan for her ideal company, she and her second husband, George Hallenbeck, planned to start Mary Kay Cosmetics. However, one month before they were to start the company, Hallenbeck died of a heart attack. It was one month after his death, when she was 45 years old, and with her young son, Richard Rogers, taking her late husband's place, that Ash started Mary Kay Cosmetics.

Mary Kay Ash came up against the extremely difficult test of starting a company and, at the same time, experiencing the death of her spouse and business partner. Just as she was forced to contend with something unexpected in fulfilling her vision, we will be forced to contend with unexpected challenges too. Hopefully our challenges won't be at the same degree of difficulty, but we can all learn from her example. We can learn to persevere from where we start in our marriage and move forward in the midst of adversity.

We start with a decisively indicative test—a litmus test of marrying well, that continues with the marital relationship. If you are going to have success in your corporate marriage, you *both* better have married well. The day-to-day choices that are made in your marriage affect everything that will challenge you in your life as a Corporate Wife. You will be affected by such choices as where you live, how you live, whom your decisions affect, who is affected by how you spend your time—these are just a snippet of the choices that become a part of, and lie beneath the surface of, your Corporate Wife Life. You can't lean on your own understanding of everything that you encounter. You have to be at peace with the notion that many choices will be made for you because you aren't driving solo behind the wheel.

But the life of a Corporate Wife is neither all about her husband nor all about her husband calling all the shots. It is about the woman behind the scenes of every shot. It is about the woman who isn't in the spotlight. This woman who isn't grandstanding to be in the spotlight is not merely a character. She is someone WITH character. And there lies the distinction. The definition of character is the way someone thinks, feels, and behaves: someone's personality. As Audrey Hepburn once said, "The true beauty in a woman is reflected in her soul."

If I had to sum up the single most important thing you should remember about your role as a Corporate Wife in a word, it would be this—*character*. Here are ten *secrets* that highlight the character of the Kick-Ass Corporate Wife.

Secret #1: The Kick-Ass Corporate Wife Is SUPPORTIVE.

Definition of "supportive": providing encouragement or emotional help.

When my husband and I got married, I knew his career involved being part of a successful family business in another city. So one of the first ways I needed to be supportive of my husband was in agreeing to where we would live. It was hard to accept that I would need to leave the city where I had lived for many years. However, because the office headquarters was located two hours north and down a winding mountain road through the foothills from my husband's home, we agreed that his mountain home would become our home base. It made the most sense for us to make this decision for a variety of reasons. However, none of those reasons had anything to do with me.

When I made the choice to be a supportive wife, I knew there would undoubtedly be times when I would have to rise above a variety of challenges in my marriage. At this time, when my marriage was new, we both understood that we couldn't continue making life decisions as individuals. My ability to make logical decisions together with my husband was essential. Even when the outcome wasn't the result of my top choice, it was often the best route to take. So, even if the reasons for these challenges had nothing to do with me, I chose to be supportive.

You Gotta Have Faith.

It wasn't always easy to see the "big picture" or to bite my tongue and to look beyond challenges that put me in conflict with my dreams. But rising above these challenges enabled me to provide positive support that not only helped him; it helped us! I learned that there is a caveat to being supportive. The caveat is that I did not immediately see how being supportive helped me.

The Secret behind Being Supportive: *Obviously being supportive helps HIM, but in the end, it also helps YOU, which means it supports your US.*

Being a supportive Corporate Wife can make you feel good about yourself because you're doing what's, supposedly, the right thing to do as a wife.

The problem with being supportive is that no matter how good that makes you feel about yourself for doing the right thing, it doesn't mean challenges won't come your way. As a married couple, challenges will come.

Back when you were single, you met challenges head-on and made decisions on your own. Now that you're married, you have to make decisions together. This sounds easy and obvious from the standpoint of marital logic. However, when it comes to the standpoint of emotion, it's something different altogether. Why? Because, at some point, you and your husband are going to have to take a stance regarding a challenging decision about which you both may not agree but a decision has to be made. Between the two of you, someone has to choose the direction to go, and you might not agree OR feel very excited about it.

What I didn't KNOW, when this decision was made to live in the location close to his work, was that I would end up discovering that by being supportive of my husband's decision, the remote mountain location would become my haven of creativity. This decision, unbeknownst to me at the time, helped me have a place of solitude—a place to think, be creative, explore, and develop my untapped potential—and to create a life I love.

What's my point in telling you this?

You don't know what you don't know.

I promise you that you don't have to fight the current of the difficult decision that someone else needs to make. I promise that if you are open to being supportive and if you are open to letting the outcome of the decision unfold, then it will! When life is viewed from an open-handed perspective (vs. holding on tight), it can free up amazing, unexpected things.

In "biting my tongue," which means, in the back of my mind I'm thinking, "What am I doing here? My dream isn't to be living here, etc., etc.," instead, I say to myself, "It's not all about ME anymore."

Isn't this what this means when you say, "I do"?

It's not about YOU. Instead of it being about YOU . . .

—It's now about you and your husband—your US.

—It's now about you and others, perhaps, if you have them, your children or stepchildren.

—It's now about more than just immediate family. It's about EMPLOYEES and CLIENTS too.

In a family business, we are responsible for people whose livelihoods depend on us. There are people who care for our property. There are people who wake up to drive to our offices all over the world. There are people, who for the past 25 years or more, have put their blood, sweat, and tears into this business that I am now connected to through saying, "I do."

Where I am and what I am doing is connected to a bigger picture, beyond me.

Where you are and what you are doing is connected to a bigger picture, beyond you.

Pause and Consider

- What are you connected to, as a Corporate Wife, that is bigger than you? What do you need to do and what can you do—to be supportive?

- What is something that you might be "fighting the current" about with your husband and not being supportive about?

- Be willing to consider the possibility that:

    o You don't know what you don't know.

    o You can apply big-picture thinking.

    o You can choose to BE supportive.

Kick-Ass Side Note—The Do & The Don't

DON'T DO THIS: Don't get caught fighting the current—it's exhausting.

DO THIS: Do think beyond yourself to discover your "big picture."

By being SUPPORTIVE, YOU might learn something you don't know that will apply to YOUR big picture, and YOU will end up being the one who is the most supported! This is how being supportive can end up helping YOU.

Secret #2: The Kick-Ass Corporate Wife Is EDUCATED.

Definition of "educated": having been informed, literate, schooled, well read, knowledgeable, enlightened.

As Kevin and I made a quick transition into our remote mountain home, many changes were happening. I wasn't aware of how this environmental relocation would affect me initially. The commute this move created turned out to be my first big challenge.

I wasn't used to being in a home that required me to commute a long distance just to get to the freeway. The freeway was the mid-point to everywhere else I needed to go. This commute didn't include cell phone coverage because it was a winding road through a remote, mountainous area. I tried to limit my trips up and down the hill by being as organized as possible. No matter how organized I tried to be, I inevitably would forget an ingredient at the grocery store for the dinner we were going to cook, or my husband would need something at the last minute that he forgot to take to the office.

As I found myself continually getting frustrated by this drive, one day it dawned on me that I could use the commute time to my advantage. I was so tired of listening to mind-numbing news or repetitive music on the radio that I decided it was time to start doing something different.

University on Wheels

One day while I was out shopping, I picked up a copy of *Success Magazine* at a local bookstore. At this time, I was not necessarily the target audience for *Success Magazine*. But I knew I couldn't continue as a frustrated, commuting Corporate Wife. So, knowing that each monthly publication included a free, enclosed CD, I purchased the magazine and played the CD in my car. The CD included recorded conversations between Darren Hardy, at the time the publisher of *Success*, and three interesting people, doing interesting things. These people were sharing amazing stories. It was as if I were surrounded by interesting people and becoming actively engaged in the conversation.

I listened repeatedly to the CD for the next 30 days. Every time I got in the car, it started to play. I picked up on something new with each listen. Over time, the content started to affect my mindset in a positive way. When the next publication was to come out at the beginning of the month, I went back to the bookstore and bought my copy. I repeated this process the next month. And the next. The content on these CDs put me back on a personal development track that I'd previously followed during my professional career. I had completely forgotten how effective it was to my mindset to include time for personal development in my life.

It didn't happen overnight, but the compounded effect of listening to these interviews over the course of time changed my perspective. I actually looked forward to my commutes!

Not only was I learning from some of the most successful people in the world, I was starting to apply their suggestions. The saying goes that you become the equivalent of the five people you hang out with every day. Even though I was alone during most of these drives, I was becoming *more* as a person. I was improving myself through the suggestions of these amazing individuals I was listening to—and hanging out with—in my car. An ancient Proverb states, *If you walk with the wise, you will become wise.* I believe the same applies when you drive with the wise!

I was flooding my mind with applicable content I could utilize in a variety of ways in my role as a Corporate Wife. Without realizing it, I was giving myself a free education.

My formerly frustrating commutes in the car became a time of inspiration, motivation, education, and mental creativity. I think every Kick-Ass Corporate Wife could benefit from making personal development a daily habit. It's a great way to gain unique access to various forms of intelligent support.

The Secret behind Being Educated: *Being educated helps YOU, but in the end, it also helps HIM, which means it supports your US.*

Most people in the dating world want to attract a future mate. I'm not referring merely to physical attraction. I'm also referring to intellectual attraction. The stereotypical dumb blonde, male or female, only goes so far in the dating realm.

The problem with the Corporate Wife is that no matter how smart she is, if she doesn't keep up with educating herself, she can lose her ability to remain intellectually attractive to the person she has attracted—her husband.

I spent so much time alone—commuting by car, traveling by plane, at home alone while my husband was traveling, alone with my television or alone shopping. I determined that I could use this time to educate myself, to get inspired, to activate my mental state so that I could develop myself personally—*How do I keep myself positive, inspired, and educated in my downtime so that it fits into my schedule easily and compounds over time into something meaningful and worthwhile, something that is intellectually stimulating to myself and others?*

No matter how busy you may be as a Corporate Wife, I promise that if you look closely at your schedule, of all of the hours in your day, you will find some downtime. You can use that downtime to your advantage. What time do you have, in the course of your day, that is downtime? Now, you may say that you're busy and have none, but consider drive time, fly time, sitting in front of the TV time, or shopping mindlessly online or at the mall time.

I'm not saying you have to fill up every waking moment of your day with noise. Downtime can even be something that happens while you're doing something else! Your weekly or bi-monthly manicure and pedicure is downtime!

Pause and Consider

- If you are not currently focusing on developing yourself personally, what amount of time can you easily fit into your schedule to become more educated and develop yourself?

- Be willing to consider the possibility that:

    o You could slip on a pair of earbuds to educate yourself with a ten- to twenty-minute podcast.

    o You can listen to something motivational during a short drive in the car by yourself.

    o You can carry a charged-up Kindle in your handbag to read something positive and educational in a moment of downtime.

Kick-Ass Side Note—The Do & The Don't

DON'T DO THIS: Don't spend countless quality hours being entertained.

DO THIS: Do use downtime wisely and invest in your own education.

What could happen if Corporate Wives around the world would replace a small portion of the time spent watching the news or reading mindless celebrity gossip magazines with personal development education? There are a lot of women, spending a lot of time, sitting idle in the lobbies of medical offices around the world these days. There are countless "beauty is pain" procedures going on at numerous offices of "physicians of perpetual youth" . . .

By being EDUCATED, you don't have to go back to a traditional classroom. You can fit education time into your daily schedule. By accessing intelligent forms of support, YOU will develop yourself personally, YOU will have a more positive mindset, and YOU will remain intellectually attractive to everyone around you, especially your husband (and yourself!). This is how being educated supports YOU.

Secret #3: The Kick-Ass Corporate Wife Is COURAGEOUS.

Definition of "courageous": not deterred by danger or pain; brave, fearless, valiant, bold.

Living alone in a community you love is altogether different from living alone in a community where you have no community. Whether you live in a remote place in the mountains or a bustling neighborhood, having no community can be a little scary. Initially, I wasn't very brave. If my husband gave me his schedule and I knew he was going to be gone for three days or more, I would pack my bags and, with my dog, hightail it down the freeway to our beach house until he returned from his business trip.

Ultimately, I was not embracing change, and I was challenged by fear. The mountain house had a lot more space than our beach home. I didn't consider myself to be a scaredy cat, but if my husband was traveling and I was alone, listening to wildlife sounds outside at night (like coyotes howling) or the sounds inside (like the crackling expansion and contraction of the wood in our ceiling) spooked me! It even spooked my growling dog!

It didn't help that scary movie commercials would inevitably appear on TV after 8:00 pm while I was innocently watching a funny talk show or comedy series. When these scary commercials came on—usually with the creepy sound of a child singing in the background—I could not grab the television remote fast enough! It was unnerving.

Scary movies and creepy sounds aside, the real fear that I was experiencing was caused by something else. I did not want to stay alone in the mountain house because I feared losing my beach community and lifestyle. I was holding on tight. If my husband was traveling, I was packing my bags too and heading to the beach for fun in the sun. Why should I be the only one to stay home alone? The truth is, my travel schedule was becoming as grueling as his. At times, I wasn't even hurrying back when he returned from his travels! This wasn't fair to him, our marriage, our dog, or me.

It took me time to consider that when he's away traveling on business, he isn't always at dinners at great restaurants. He isn't always playing golf or relaxing in the sun on a sport fishing tournament. Most times, he is making difficult decisions, in a different time zone, while staying in an unfamiliar hotel environment. The last thing my husband wants to come home to after a long business trip is an empty mountain house. Do I really want to trade places with him? No. Do I want him to feel a peace of mind while he is at work, slaying the dragons, not having to worry about "little ole me" back at home, being a shrinking violet of some kind? Yes.

From an outsider's perspective, I was living the Corporate Wife's lifestyle of abundance. From my internal perspective, all that abundance was clouded by a mindset focused on all of the things I didn't have, also known as a scarcity mindset. I was living in fear and holding on tightly to some semblance of my previous life. Perhaps this was due to all of the changes I was experiencing so quickly as a new wife, in a new role, in an unfamiliar environment. Understandably, I wanted to maintain my sense of community and belonging by holding onto the comforting feelings of familiarity.

As time went on, however, I realized that this scenario was not working for me, my husband, or even my community of friends at the beach. Rightly so, my friends were not as readily available to be with me on my ever-changing commute timetable. Now it seemed as if something had shifted. Everyone's lives were changing, all of a sudden, and it wasn't as easy to count on these times of fun and familiarity. I was losing my comfort zone.

House to Home

As motivational speaker Tony Robbins says, "Every problem has a solution." My husband and I realized that we needed to do something about our mountain house. We needed to make it our mountain HOME. After we were married, I had moved into "his house," but it didn't have a feeling that it was "our home."

It was during this time that we took simple steps to determine how our individual design sensibilities could work together in unison to create a home environment we both loved and wanted to live in. Fortunately, we had similar tastes in interior colors, furniture, design, and style!

Just because I moved into his house, it didn't initially make it my "home." In my scenario, it created my scarcity mindset because his home was something that didn't belong to me. It was his. In order for me to be comfortable, what was his needed to become OURS, and that took some courage to figure out and make a reality. Once we did, I could move from fear and a mindset of scarcity to one of peace and living abundantly. With a newfound discovery of our "home" and choosing to look at it in the mindset of abundance, this present and now "future home" could become bigger than this house of the past. When you have this kind of mindset, you'll think, *Eureka! I won't even need to seek out a quick tutorial on burning sage to purify this home of past negative energies!*

The Secret behind Being Courageous: *Being courageous helps HIM by giving him peace of mind, but in the end, it also helps YOU, which means it supports your US.*

The necessity of making your future bigger than your past is something that, at some point, you will need to address on your life's journey. It takes courage, and having courage is a requirement to move forward. It takes courage to move forward into a place you've never been before.

The problem with moving forward and making the future bigger is that it is kind of scary because it's unknown. But to move forward with courage, you must start with the future as the lead.

You must go forward with a step. With simple steps toward determining, creating, and paying attention to the sensibilities of who you are and what you love, you then establish the foundations for the future life you will love even more as each day moves forward.

I promise you that if you look at your life and your marriage from the standpoint that you are setting yourself up to be okay, or at least as okay as you can be, to move forward, you will be better prepared for the unknown. This all falls under the area of courage.

If you take care of yourself and your surroundings as a Corporate Wife, to create a life that is continually propelling you to think and move forward—meaning you are developing yourself personally and cultivating interests outside of your marriage, at the same time, in the context of your marriage, you will be doing your best to set yourself up for success for whatever life brings your way. You will be saving yourself hours, days, weeks, months, and years worth of standing still in fear, complaints, or confusion. You will be developing your courage muscles.

Pause and Consider

- What's not working for you in your life right now? Where do you need to dig in and apply your courage?

- If you are struggling with something that you want to complain to your girlfriends about every single time they call you and you can't get past this supposed problem, I propose that you think about this thing— what is it about this "thing" that may be developing, that is out of your comfort zone to solve? Where are you out of your comfort zone? Where are you thinking in terms of scarcity? Remember, this is your life! It's your time to dig deep and find your courage. Time is of the essence. The time to get started is now.

- To be blunt, THIS is the time to be *a LOT more KICK-ASS!*

- Consider the possibility that:

  ○ Your vision needs to be bigger.

  ○ You can reverse engineer it.

  ○ You can start with the first baby step.

Kick-Ass Side Note—The Do & The Don't

DON'T DO THIS: Don't think small—think big picture!

DO THIS: Do start with one baby step toward your vision.

Here's what I propose: look at a situation where you need courage from a "big picture" point of view. If you could wave your magic wand with what you have in your hands, what would you like it to look like? Now that you know the outcome, turn it around. Look at it in a reverse-engineered fashion, and work backwards. When you get to the first step, start there. By being courageous, YOU start with taking a baby step toward your goal of living the rest of your life with a mindset filled with abundance. This is how being courageous supports YOU.

Secret #4: The Kick-Ass Corporate Wife Is CREATIVE.

Definition of "creative": involving the imagination or original ideas, especially in the production of an artistic work.

When we started blending our individual home design sensibilities, I started considering ways to improve our home by collating our ideas into an idea book. Whenever I saw a photo that resonated with me in an interior design magazine, I ripped out the page and put it in my idea book. From time to time, we would look through this book to determine if there was any continual thread, or pattern, that weaved through ideas and reflected "us." I knew we had to get rid of the former man cave motifs that were not acceptable to our vision of "us."

We ended up learning about each other's tastes and preferences through this process. For instance, we both prefer clean lines with modern and traditional elements. By keeping things structured and non-decorative, which is our preference, we could begin to add elements of art and artifacts later on that we found in our travels or spotted when *together.*

Some of our shared ideas were going to take time to implement—especially where actual construction would be involved—but we created a plan, over time, and stuck to it. Eventually, this project became a pathway for me to take the focus off my fear. The saying is true that fear is just an acronym for **F**alse **E**vidence **A**ppearing **R**eal. The false evidence in my mind was that I was losing my beach lifestyle. The reality—and not just an appearance of something real—was that I was gaining another option! It was not the scarcity equation of $1 + 1 = 1$. It was the equation showing me that $1 + 1 =$ even more than 2—it equals an abundant life!

An additional home isn't necessary to add something to life to feel a sense of "addition" in this situation. I embraced what was in front of me: I had a *house* in the mountains, but now I was an active participant in its reinvention. Now, our mountain *home* had the possibility of becoming an additional place for all of us that inhabits a sense of community, belonging, and love.

The Secret behind Being Creative (with "creative" referring to creating a sense of union, belonging, and love): *Being creative helps HIM to rest assured that his decision for you two to live in his house (or live in his state/city/area, etc.) isn't just him pushing his life onto you on his terms; instead, being creative helps him see your buy-in and commitment to your new life together as a* *couple—and it helps YOU in the same way. It propels the US in your marriage.*

How are you and your husband going to ensure that you pursue a shared creative vision? How will you commune and compare both your ideas?

This is what Kevin and I are doing to pursue a shared vision for our home.

We are at the place where we are making strides in figuring out what we want to do with our home, and using our idea book to help us see over the course of time, patterns of things that we both find appealing. We have gathered enough of this "evidence" to be at the point where we can share our vision with our contractor and his team, and get their take on some upcoming projects.

Once you and your spouse sketch out that shared vision of any big project, a vision that incorporates both your ideas, then the next step is implementation. However, something to consider with a massive project is that it isn't going to complete itself overnight. So the important thing we had to determine was how to break it up into manageable pieces and how to sequence them—which piece to begin with, move to next, and finally end with. We decided to start with one portion of our goal and work on one section at a time, based on what was most important to us and our lifestyle. We chose initially to work on the fireplace in the living room.

You need to break creative projects into chunks that are easily measurable. Especially in the course of marriage, a big project like the construction of a home is STRESSFUL. If your goal is to creatively and intentionally make your house a home or community, determine where a good starting point is for you to build community within your home. For us, that meant the living room. We wanted to create a comfortable, cozy spot, where we wouldn't have a TV, where we could rest, relax, and enjoy conversation or silence. In working on this project, in one area, our entire home wasn't disrupted.

Pause and Consider

- I promise that if you really think about how you and your husband can creatively come up with a simple strategy to determine what you both love and where you can create a place to love, with a little time and attention, it will happen.

- Start looking for a medium to collect resources that will accumulate in your own idea book, vision board, or online—a Pinterest page.

- Consider the possibility that:

   o You can tap into your creative style by looking at a variety of things you love.

   o You can also tap into your creative style by recognizing what you don't like.

   o Make it easy and arrange both your ideas in one cohesive place and get continual feedback on it.

Kick-Ass Side Note—The Do & The Don't

DON'T DO THIS: Don't get stuck on the realistic—this is a time to have fun and dream.

DO THIS: Do add involvement photos, for example, a photo of you reading a book in a gorgeous new chair or you and your husband seated at a beautiful new table, instead of just furniture photos.

Here's an easy way to start: pick up three things:

- Hardbound, blank book at the art supply store

- Glue stick

- Pen

Tear out magazine photos. Pick up fabric samples and paint color swatches. Visit furniture stores together on a weekend and have some fun! Collect alternating photos of you and your husband, pretending you're reading while sitting in a gorgeous chair you both find appealing. Go to town in your book, no holds barred. Print out your photos and review your idea book together. Soon, you'll be adding receipts for items you've purchased, and before you know it, your idea book will be overflowing with ideas that came from both of you. By being creative, YOU contribute to developing your new, unique style as a couple together, making your house a home. This is how being creative supports YOU.

Secret #5: The Kick-Ass Corporate Wife Is CONTENT.

Definition of "content": in a state of peaceful happiness, satisfied, pleased, fulfilled, happy, cheerful.

As a couple of years progressed in our mountain home, I began to pay closer attention to the way that we lived inside our home. I was happy with what we were doing to create all of the positive changes, but something was missing. I couldn't put my finger on it at first.

When I'd unpack my books or papers onto the kitchen table every day, my husband noticed that I had no place to call my own. It may sound strange that I couldn't find space within a large home with plenty of square footage. But the issue was that I didn't have my own designated personal space. My husband had his "man cave" room, which included a bar, his personal library, and all of his fishing expedition memorabilia. We had additional bedrooms, a video game room, and even a separate room for visiting guests. Without intruding on the spaces already designated for others, I didn't have an area that was my own space.

I needed space, and I didn't have it. I needed my own space, a place to feel at peace. As Virginia Woolf described it, "A Room of One's Own." There are many things that can cause feelings of discontentment in marriage, and my living space is just one example.

Feeling content with your surroundings is different than being content with exterior forces over which you have no control. For example, I think it feels really good when someone remembers me on my birthday. When someone calls or sends a card or a gift, it's a blessing. On the flip side, when someone doesn't remember, especially a family member or good friend, it can be disappointing. I can't be responsible if you happen to forget my birthday. I can't control your actions or behaviors. If I feel a great sense of discontentment that you forgot, I can do something to assist in the outcome next year by reminding you beforehand.

But feeling content about my surroundings was something that I had to recognize and learn that I could control, and create, with the help of my husband, for the benefit of both of us.

No Place to Call My Own

Yes, I could go outside and go for a walk and find my space, like at our outdoor pond filled with koi, trout, turtles, and all kinds of wildlife, thus providing solace. Inside the house, I could shut the bathroom door and take a bath for some space. However, my husband wanted me to truly feel content in our home. He made me realize that we could create a space just for me where I could let my hair down, where I could leave the room as it was. A room that didn't change unless I changed it. If I set down a piece of paper— or even a pile of papers—it wouldn't move unless I said so.

Having my own space could provide me with a sense of peace. I could have a place to go that would make me feel content. Within my own designated space I could feel content enough to realize that any realm of any possibility might exist.

Creating Spaces I Love

Kevin and I began to notice the areas in our home that we rarely used. We had always done our best to not make big changes in our home because we wanted the kids to have a home that looked familiar. But they had clearly outgrown the zebra-themed playroom . . .

It didn't happen overnight, due to the amount of construction involved, but we created a space for me out of the playroom. My new personal space included a new desk, a chair, a window, and my own closet with a keypad lock. The space even had glass doors that could shut if needed. This new space opened the door for me to have a place to go to dream, create, and develop my vision for my business—and my life. It also just gives me a place where I don't have to worry that someone else is involved. It's my sacred ground. It's a place where I find contentment.

And with my own space, we began to notice the increased amount of time I was spending at our mountain home. I was still visiting our beach home from time to time, but I was falling in love with our mountain home and embracing our remote mountain lifestyle.

I believe every woman needs a place in her home where she can feel content and at peace, where she can truly feel at home. The key is to be content with the process—remember, *it is an unfolding*—and to find contentment in the place where you land.

The Secret behind Being Content: *Being content helps HIM by giving him peace of mind about you, but in the end, it also helps YOU, which means it supports your US.*

How do you find contentment? How do you find your sense of personal space? Is it important to you to have a place where you can be alone and feel totally at ease being alone?

If you are someone who is not self-aware, who is not paying attention to how you maneuver through your house, you may find yourself moving things from place to place. Or, perhaps YOU are moving from place to place. Constant transition, within one's home, makes it hard to feel at peace. It makes it hard to want to be there.

Pause and Consider

- I promise that if you look for a small space of some kind and put the energy into transforming it into a place you can call your own, it will enhance your life and the lives of those around you. It doesn't necessarily require construction; perhaps, it's just a desk in the corner of a room. It's a place where you can go to do what you want to do.

- I propose that once you find your place, a place where you can safely land and go to on a regular basis:

  o You will find a sense of contentment.

  o You will discover a greater sense of inner peace that you wouldn't have found otherwise.

  o You will learn how to create boundaries around your space and receive the respect you need for your private time.

Kick-Ass Side Note—The Do & The Don't

DON'T DO THIS: Don't let contentment become an excuse to be complacent.

DO THIS: Do create a space for yourself that is solely for you to enjoy.

Have you ever considered where you might want to create your sense of personal space to find contentment? My mother used to go downstairs to our basement and sit under one of those big, old-fashioned hairdryers to dry her hair and read. Looking back at this, I now realize that having her own personal space must have given her a great sense of contentment (and the ability to block out the noise of five crazy kids!) Whether it's a room, a desk, or a hairdryer, consider creating a place for yourself. Feeling content in your home will overflow into all areas of your life. This is how being content supports YOU.

Secret #6: The Kick-Ass Corporate Wife Is AMBITIOUS.

Definition of "ambitious": Having or showing a strong desire and determination to succeed, enterprising, aspiring, enthusiastic, committed, a plan intended to satisfy high aspirations and therefore difficult to achieve.

They say, *The way to a man's heart is through his stomach.* The problem with this theory, as far as my husband is concerned, is that I came into this marriage with a "single girl's" mentality regarding "dinner." I learned quickly that my husband would not be satisfied with my version of dinner: a protein bar and a glass of red wine.

When the weather turned cold, I found that I enjoyed nesting at home. It was not a common occurrence, but on one particularly chilly day, I pulled the *Williams-Sonoma Essentials of Healthful Cooking* cookbook out of the cupboard. I wanted to find a recipe to surprise my husband with a home-cooked meal. I am not a good cook. In fact, I am much more of a baker than someone who cooks meat. The only way I can cook meat is if it's placed in a baking dish in the oven, or perhaps in a slow cooking crockpot. Knowing my limitations, I spotted a main dish recipe that looked like it would be doable. It was a recipe on page 122 in the chicken section. The title was "Coq au Vin."

I promise you, I'm not a culinary whiz. Prior to this day, I had never made, or even eaten, "coq au vin."

Working with Your Limitations

French recipe, complicated or not, I believed I had enough ambition to easily make this "chicken in wine." I had all the ingredients, the proper cookware, and the time to create (what I hoped would be) a masterpiece. I was excited at the possibility of surprising my husband when he came through the door, with the aroma of a delicious, home-cooked meal.

The recipe called for a variety of ingredients—pearl onions, baby artichokes, preservative-free bacon, and cremini mushrooms, to name a few. Some were cooked for five minutes here, five minutes there. Then the bacon was fried, and the chicken was seared. I was managing the process surprisingly well. Once the chicken was to return to my Le Creuset dutch oven to simmer in wine and broth, it had another 1 to 1.25 hours to go. This amount of time would be just perfect for Kevin to arrive home while it was still cooking. We could enjoy a pre-dinner salad, some fine wine, and romantic candlelight.

The Secret behind Being Ambitious: *Being ambitious helps HIM by surprising and delighting him with aspects of you he may not yet know, but in the end, it also helps YOU, which means it supports your US.*

If you've never done something as ambitious as cooking a recipe that seems to be a little outside of your comfort zone, I encourage you to do so. Skydiving, yoga, mixed martial arts, hip-hop dancing, reading all the books in the *Lord of the Rings* trilogy, learning a foreign language—whatever you want! If you have the strong desire to satisfy a high aspiration, jump in and do it!

Pause and Consider

- I promise that getting a little ambitious and trying something new—whether it be for an afternoon at home with YouTube videos as the instructor or a weekend retreat with a coach and some others—will surprise and delight you. You'll reconnect with the childlike, eager-to-learn parts of yourself. And your husband will be amazed and delighted with your daring and multidimensionality.

- Consider the possibility that:

  - You have the determination to succeed at something that's a little difficult (or uncomfortable) to achieve.

  - You have what it takes to discover a hidden or dormant talent.

  - You have the ability to delight yourself and impress others when you exercise your ambition.

Kick-Ass Side Note—The Do & The Don't

DON'T DO THIS: Don't let intimidation negatively affect your self-imposed limitations.

DO THIS: Do have a determination to succeed at something challenging.

By being ambitious, your efforts will pay off in ways you may never have expected—as you'll see in part two of my "coq au vin" saga (see Secret #7). You will soon learn the rest of the story regarding how being ambitious helps YOU.

Secret #7: The Kick-Ass Corporate Wife Is GOOD-NATURED.

Definition of "good-natured": kind, friendly, patient, warm-hearted, amiable.

Kevin arrived home a little early, but his words were music to my ears. "It smells wonderful! What's for dinner, sweetie?"

"Coq au vin," I revealed proudly, and as nonchalantly as if I'd said, "Kentucky Fried Chicken."

"Wow—that's impressive!" he admitted. "How much longer is it supposed to cook?"

"A little less than an hour," I replied. "If you're hungry now, we can sit down and enjoy some wine with our dinner salads while it finishes up cooking."

As we sat at the dinner table, discussing his day while enjoying our wine and salads, we started to smell something burning. Soon it smelled like smoke. I walked over to the oven and lifted the lid of the dutch oven.

I lowered the lid, noting, "Hmmm . . . something's not right."

He came over, peered into the dutch oven, and then declared, "Oh no! The bottom of the pan is scorched! Sweetie, when you use these cast iron pans, you have to cook on the lowest setting because they get very hot."

I looked inside the pan. The bottom of the dutch oven was burnt, covered in black, and ruined. The chicken, which was meant to be marinating in juices, was completely charred, dry, and shriveled up.

Exasperated, I pulled the meat out of the pan with tongs and placed each lonely piece on our individual dinner plates. Our coq au vin was coq au disaster! It looked like two pieces of dried up carcass. As I served the plate to my husband, he observed that there was a remaining baguette sitting on the kitchen counter.

"What's the bread for, sweetie?" he inquired, hopefully.

"That bread was to be served with our chicken. It was supposed to soak up the juices from the pan."

We sat at the table, looking down at our individual carcasses in silence. My eyes started to well up with tears. I felt like such a failure! I had tried so hard to make the perfect dinner all by myself.

"I'm sorry, sweetie," he offered, trying to comfort me.

Our dinner was not even edible.

I stood up, marched our plates to the kitchen, and dumped all of the evidence of this disastrous meal into the trash compactor.

I grabbed a second bottle of wine out of the pantry, yanked out the cork, and brought it back to the table—to sulk and drown my sorrows into my glass of French red.

As we lifted our glasses to make a toast to the hope of tomorrow's dinner meal—the kitchen dinger suddenly went off.

"What's that alarm for?" my husband asked.

"Well, that's the amount of time the chicken was supposed to cook!"

At that, we both cracked up laughing.

The Secret behind Being Good-Natured: *Being good-natured and being able to laugh at yourself helps HIM because he can see that you have a sense of self-deprecating humor. In the words of Robert Frost, "If we couldn't laugh, we would all go insane."* Marriage is serious business. It's important to take your marriage seriously and your role as a Corporate Wife seriously, but the way to do that is to not take *yourself* too seriously.

Pause and Consider

- I promise that by lightening up and recognizing how to laugh at yourself, you'll be able to leap over the messes of life—or the messed-up meals. Humor can be found in almost any situation. You'll learn how to turn stressful scenarios into stories that "you'll laugh about later." Your husband will appreciate that you're not miserable to be around in these types of situations, and he'll look forward to participating in the success of the story when you try again and triumph! Make a little fun of yourself and win over your audience of one: your husband.

- Consider the possibility that:

  - You have the capacity to lighten up and laugh at yourself now and then.

  - You have my permission to not live up to your own perception of perfection.

  - You have the choice to have FUN in your role, even if it requires a little elbow grease to clean up the mess. (And as my dutch oven needed, elbow grease + baking soda + a few days of soaking!)

Kick-Ass Side Note—The Do & The Don't

DON'T DO THIS: Don't take yourself too seriously and expect perfection.

DO THIS: Do have fun in your role and laugh at yourself WITH your husband.

By being able to laugh at yourself, you'll learn that in spite of your best intentions, things don't always work out as planned. Page 122 of our *Williams-Sonoma* cookbook now has the word "Disaster!" written with a bold blue sharpie at the bottom of the page, along with an underlined "simmer."

Even though this meal will go down in history as a disaster, I promise you that it's one of the stories we love to refer to and laugh about often.

Thankfully, all was not lost: I'm happy to report that the dutch oven was saved.

Secret #8: The Kick-Ass Corporate Wife Is CONFIDENT.

Definition of "confident": self-assured, positive, assertive, self-reliant, poised.

Personality tests are interesting because they reveal your strengths and your limitations. The problem though, with personality tests, is that they reveal your strengths and your limitations. It's all fun and games when strengths are revealed as you're comparing your personality type to that of your favorite breed of dog. It's not as fun when you see who you really are and your limitations get magnified.

I'm so grateful to report that I have learned, through the revelation of personality test results, that I married someone with many strengths. He has strengths where I have limitations, and vice versa. My strengths lie in areas that are different than his, and that's how we balance each other out. It's not something that causes me jealousy. It's something I choose to celebrate. When other people notice, I am content to let my husband shine in the spotlight.

A simplistic, but related, example is my husband's knowledge of minutia. For example, he is the type of guy who can answer nearly every question on *Jeopardy*. I consider it a good night if I can answer two or three questions! Does that leave me feeling less-than or like I have to compete with him? No. It just shows me that we are different, and it helps me celebrate that he's the fun, "smarty pants" *Jeopardy* guy. I don't love *Jeopardy*, but he does, and I love high-fiving him when he gets the right answer (and razzing him when he doesn't!). To have an understanding regarding why we operate the way we do, and that we are created the way we are, is very helpful and freeing. It creates balance in our relationship.

Competition during a game can be fun now and then, but unhealthy competition within a marriage can cause a lot of problems. If you don't have a healthy sense of self-confidence, and you're not at ease with your husband being in the spotlight—whatever kind of spotlight that may be—it can disrupt the equilibrium that made your differences a good thing for the two of you as a couple.

To enhance your self-confidence, or even to express it, you may find yourself taking on a new challenge. And if you are taking on a new challenge, such as waking up at the crack of dawn to start a new workout program or something that is going to require a change in your usual behavior or schedule, this needs to be thought out with care. Keeping your priorities in place when taking on something new will eliminate a strain on your schedule or an unhealthy competition within your marriage. It requires being intentional about keeping your act—and your new act—together, and all together. It can be done, but it might not be done in the way you plan, so make room for contingencies. It won't support either of you if you're exhausted and asleep by 7 pm or at a time you might usually spend together.

A new habit, goal, or dream of yours might be something new to your husband. Chances are, he will embrace what you want to do, but also he might be concerned about how this new thing will change the dynamics of your relationship. Tread lightly, tread carefully, and pay attention to your priorities. Map them out and determine what is most important in your relationship. You may find that the more you have to do, the more you actually accomplish! When you find yourself being more productive in a positive way, it can be a huge confidence booster.

One way that you can improve your sense of self-confidence is by getting a better understanding of who you really are and what makes you tick. Investigate some personality tests that reveal more about you. Share your findings with a good friend and—if you're willing—your husband. It might be helpful to both of you to know more about each other so that you can operate from new levels of understanding.

You can be confident in who you are and who your husband is, and agree to accept the differences and work with those differences. You both don't have to fight the current, or compete within the current. Confidence comes from feeling secure in your identity as a person, with or without your husband. It doesn't operate from the standpoint of fierce independence or cowardly bravado.

I like to think of confidence as not shrinking. As the saying goes, *Your playing small doesn't serve the world*. I also like the analogy of a firm hand in a velvet glove. As a confident Corporate Wife, you can exude light and love in a way that emits a quiet strength that is contagious to others.

It doesn't mean you have to play a game of superiority, but it does mean you can be cool, calm, and collected—empowered with inner strength and maturity. It's not about perfection, but a personality that is more about sunny skies than a tornado.

The Secret behind Being Confident: *Being confident in who you are helps HIM because he can be who he is, and he will appreciate that you celebrate his strengths. In doing so, he will appreciate YOUR strengths.* Your differences together make you, as a couple, more interesting and compatible.

Pause and Consider

- I promise that by being confident in yourself and embracing what makes you personally tick, you will discover how your strengths and talents culminate as a couple. It doesn't mean that you have to become strong at what the other person is strong at doing. It isn't supposed to be an unhealthy competition.

- Consider the possibility that:

  o Your individual strengths are meant to enhance your relationship.

  o Your differences bring something unique to your marriage because solid marriages rely on balance.

  o Marriage doesn't have to be a competition, but rather, a union of security that allows your confidence in one another to soar.

Kick-Ass Side Note—The Do & The Don't

DON'T DO THIS: Don't try to one-up your spouse and create a sense of unhealthy competition.

DO THIS: Do have a healthy sense of self-confidence and celebrate each other's strengths.

Consider the areas where you might feel a sense of envy in regard to something for which your husband gets praise, especially if it's from other people. Marriage isn't an arena for feelings of inadequacy regarding your partner's strengths. It's not meant to make you less of a person when your partner gets more attention than you do. By being non-competitive and celebrating the unique strengths that you both have, YOU promote acceptance and appreciation in your marriage. This is what it means to be a good sport! This is how being confident supports YOU.

Secret #9: The Kick-Ass Corporate Wife Is KIND.

Definition of "kind": generous, helpful, thinking about other people's feelings.

Don't you love it when you get a pleasant surprise? Something like an unexpected letter from a friend or a package in the mail? It's like a breath of fresh air! We get so busy in the day-to-day of everyday life that we forget the simple notion of surprising and delighting someone.

Back when I was working in sales, I can remember how we were encouraged to take something, such as cookies or a coffee, to a potential customer to set ourselves apart from the other competitors in our industry. It was always fun to show up at a client's office with food or a birthday cake at 3:00 in the afternoon. Timing is everything with sugary sweets, and I soon discovered the true meaning of the phrase "brownie points."

One day, I picked up a cup of coffee to deliver to one of my potential clients. When I got past the gatekeeper, my client said something unexpected, in confidence, related to his marriage, "In all the years I've been married, not once has my wife ever brought me a cup of coffee to the office."

Even though I was single at the time, his statement stuck with me. Granted, I was not trying to pick up on this client, and I certainly wasn't trying to cause any problems in his marriage. I was just doing my job, trying to get my foot in the door to earn his business. But it made me wonder how this man's marriage could have been transformed over something that costs less than five dollars.

When you do something to surprise and delight—it's like being a cheerful giver. You are the one who delights in the giving of the surprise, and the receiver gets to delight in the receiving of the surprise. It's a win-win that starts with a simple, perhaps random, act of kindness.

I've had conversations with men who say they love when their wives leave them surprising love notes or pop by the office with a packed lunch or who even simply ask if they would like a foot rub after a long day at work. It doesn't even cost money to be delightful and kind. It just takes a little creativity. It doesn't have to be difficult to be kind. Kindness is not reserved only for strangers.

There's a little place in our home where I like to sit each morning. It's on the couch, in front of the (propane-charged) fireplace, under the green antique lamp that belonged to my grandmother.

I like to sit and read and drink my coffee, snuggled up with my dog while my husband works out in our garage gym.

There was a time that for a few mornings, I would sit, without the cozy fireplace turned on. Its remote was somehow broken, so it couldn't be turned on.

My husband noticed that the fire wasn't burning and was disturbed by it. I didn't make a big deal of it, but when he came home from work that night, he took the fireplace apart to figure out why it wasn't turning on properly. He determined that some soot had built up by the starter. He vacuumed it up, put the fireplace back together and—*voila!*—turned it on.

I instantly declared, "*My hero! Sweetie, you are the MAN of the house! Thank you so much!*"

His chest puffed up, and he (kiddingly and teasingly) said, "*Finally! Some appreciation!*"

But I honestly meant it. He went out of his way for me, and I let him know it with kindness—a thank you can make such a positive difference in your marriage.

This is just a small example of how true, honest words of kindness and appreciation can go a long way.

Participating in random acts and words of kindness might reveal new things to you about your husband. You might see him carrying a screwdriver around the house a lot more often—just to see what he can fix!

What's even more exciting is the notion that he won't hesitate to fix something when it breaks because "you looked at it and it broke!"

The Secret behind Being Kind: *Being kind helps HIM because kindness can be random (or nonexistent) in his world if it doesn't* *come from you.* Remember how kind you were to your husband in the beginning? It's easy to lose that passion in the mundane routine of everyday life. By using a little imagination and by being kind, you BOTH win.

Pause and Consider

- If you aren't kind to your husband, you're missing out on opportunities to show the unique, creative, and fun side of your personality.

- Consider the possibility that:

  - Your husband wants to be reminded why he married YOU.

  - Your husband needs for YOU to be kind to him.

  - Your husband loves any random act of kindness, whether it's for him or for someone else because it comes from YOU.

Kick-Ass Side Note—The Do & The Don't

DON'T DO THIS: Don't miss out on opportunities to thank your husband with kindness.

DO THIS: Do something kind—some simple gesture that will surprise and delight your husband.

Our lives can get so busy, as we check off each box on our to-do list each day. Being kind doesn't need to be something that just adds more to the list. If you can't remember the last time you did something to surprise and delight your husband (meaning you've just checked your watch and can tell me the time you did something TODAY), it's time to get creative! Remember, it doesn't require money. It doesn't have to be anything big or elaborate. It just requires a little imagination . . . like scratching his back when you're in the passenger's seat!

By being kind, you're revealing your style in a way that never goes out of style. When you do something that makes your husband say, "Sweetie, what you did for me today kicks ass!" you both win. By being kind, YOU set the stage for being "that kind of person," someone who can't help but experience random acts of kindness in return. Everybody wins. This is how being kind supports YOU!

Secret #10: The Kick-Ass Corporate Wife Is CHARITABLE.

Definition of "charitable": assistance of those in need, philanthropic, humanitarian, altruistic, benevolent, generous, considerate.

When you think of the words "Corporate Wife," in the realm of charity, it conjures up a stereotypical image—the beautiful woman dressed in high heels, in the latest designer gown, professionally styled hair and makeup, cocktail in hand, schmoozing with the crowd at this week's featured charity ball. She's even featured smiling among local celebrities in the society section of your city magazine. There are many opportunities for this realm of charity in the life of the Corporate Wife. It's a wonderful thing to be able to participate in events that give to charity.

If you've grown up learning about charity in ways that differ from events like this "charity ball" description, it can be a little confusing. Perhaps you learned that charity is something done in secret. There was an understanding that when you give, you will get something back for your good deed, but you don't give *expecting* anything in return, such as an item you won because you bid on it at an auction. So, if this is how charity was explained to you, a charity ball can seem a little odd.

This is all part of the "allure" and the mystique of the Corporate Wife when it comes to charity.

The reality of being involved in a charity requires careful consideration by the Corporate Wife because she can get sucked into a vortex of volunteerism. Yes, she will be rewarded with recognition, status, and various kudos. She might get something in return for her voluntary efforts. Where you need to be careful with charity, or any endeavor that you love, is that the thing you used to love becomes the thing that loves you more. Whether it's a charity, a goal, or a business, it can drive a husband crazy when he considers the amount of time and effort his wife puts in, in exchange for what she actually gets in return.

But what about the other reality, the one with the charity the Corporate Wife is involved in where she doesn't get much, if any, recognition in return for the time she puts in? This type of charity typically begins at home.

At some point in your life as a Corporate Wife, you may have to deal with issues of an aging or potentially very ill parent. As it is with anyone you love more than anything—even a pet—no matter how much we try to tell ourselves that we know the day is coming, we can never be prepared enough for illness, aging, or the death of a loved one. The reality is that you must deal with the situation as best you can. In doing so, you probably won't get the recognition, the status, or the various kudos when you are dealing with this type of charity that begins at home. But you can be the kind of person who doesn't do it because it's all about you—because the truth is, it's not. You're not doing it because you'll be in the spotlight. You're doing it out of love and compassion. This is the heart of charity.

It's an interesting dynamic, as a Corporate Wife, when your role changes from that of a daughter to that of a caregiver. When one parent is no longer living and you are the one managing the care of the surviving parent, it can be tough, on a variety of levels, because you don't know what's going to happen. Perhaps it's going to require your surviving parent to consider a change in location to be closer to you or another family member. If space allows, it might require a temporary stay at your home for your parent to get acclimated to the loss of his or her spouse. If the move becomes more than a temporary stay, it might require your parent to make a permanent—even cross-country—move.

In our parents' world, making locational moves wasn't as common or relevant as it is today because most families lived together in the same general vicinity. They may never have had to deal with long-distance moves. The aging they've seen didn't require uprooting and dealing with full-blown change at an older age. Today, big location changes are typical for most families with an aging parent, and you, as the Corporate Wife, may find yourself in the role of managing the change either for your parent/s, or even your husband's parent/s.

Whatever the scenario with one aging parent, or two, as a charitable Corporate Wife, your role is going to evolve with a different dynamic. All of those years where your parent or parents cared for you will be flipped where you are going to have to take over that role. You have to do your homework and create a plan. You have to look at the options. You'll need to consider your parent's health and, depending on his or her age, recognize what your parent is capable of in light of the Rolodex of potential problems from bad knees to hearing loss. You'll need to ask the difficult questions that come with the options of living in your guesthouse, in a condo nearby, in a community center, or in an assisted living environment.

As a busy Corporate Wife, it will create added pressure. You may need to adjust your schedule for frequent doctor appointments and other forms of help. Whether you do it yourself or even if you hire help, you will still be involved, and it will be a test of your compassion skills. The best thing, and the right thing to do, is to figure out how you're going to fit into those big compassion shoes and prepare yourself for putting them on in a moment's notice.

When the scenario is such that both parents are still alive, you may find that one parent becomes the caretaker. This is also a scenario where you, as the Corporate Wife, will need to step in to help with the delicate task of taking hold of the reins. One fully functional parent may seem like he or she is completely capable of handling the medications or the doctor visits, but it can be very wearing on the healthier parent. There's an element of control that the healthier parent wants to keep since it's been going on for years, so it's not going to be an easy task getting his or her permission for a visiting nurse, a maid, or even a neighbor to check in to make sure everything is okay.

The best thing to do in this situation is to create the conversation. Create opportunities to share your concerns with your parents. Let the healthier parent know that he or she has your permission to ask for help. If siblings are involved, don't leave anyone out of the conversation regarding your concerns. Talk to everyone involved, and be open to their feedback. It's also vital that you communicate with care and love with your parents when having difficult conversations. No parent wants to feel like they are a burden or an inconvenience.

One time, I heard one of my favorite marketing mentors, Joe Polish, talk about how he felt that it isn't right to go to someone's funeral and speak about that person from the pulpit if those words had never been said to the person who died. His words made me think differently in terms of charity beginning at home, especially in regard to my aging parents.

I have always kept a letter that my dad typed out—and by typing, I mean pecking out the letters of a typewriter—that he sent to me shortly after my graduating from college while I was a newly working career-girl. It was evident that he'd typed it out at the end of a long workday since he put the date AND the time on the letter. I appreciated his intentions and his efforts, and it is something that continues to hold deep meaning to me. After thinking about what I would ever say about my dad, while he was living, it was evident to me that I needed to share with him that I still read this letter, how important it is for me to have it, and how much I appreciated that he wrote it.

So, on a December trip to Dallas, I brought the letter with me. I created the opportunity to pull it out and share it with both of my parents, together. My father held the letter, and even though it probably took him forty-five minutes to read what would take you or me four to five minutes max, it was a moment that made me understand the full meaning of charity beginning at home.

In fact, I even wrote Joe Polish a letter when I returned from my trip, thanking him for his suggestion and explaining how his simple suggestion made such a positive impact on my life. His suggestion generated the greatest Christmas gift for me: a memorable moment with both of my parents while they were both alive, sharing gratitude for something my father had written some twenty-five years prior that still has meaning today. (My mother was behind the typing part of it, guaranteed—because his handwriting was nearly illegible!)

When you take time to be charitable, you gain the opportunity to transcend into a higher dimension. Charity takes down walls and builds up someone's world. All that is required is that you start somewhere, and that somewhere can be within the realm of your own home and family.

Having compassion through words is a great way to start the concept of charity at home. If you can't physically be with your parents, send a card or flowers with a nice note. Buy your parents an iPad and start Facetiming or Skyping them. Look for the little things that might help both of them as individuals, but especially the caretaker parent. Whether it's something as simple as new kitchen towels, or perhaps a new flavor of coffee that they wouldn't normally buy for themselves, the important thing is to send something that lets them know you are with them in spirit.

When I got home one day, I noticed a personally addressed letter that stood out in the pile. It had a quirky little puff sticker with a guy's face on it in the upper left-hand corner. When I opened it, it was a handwritten letter from my marketing mentor, Joe Polish. It wasn't elaborate and looked as if it were written with a red Sharpie, but it was something personal, and it was from him, telling me how special it was for him to hear that he'd made a positive difference for someone.

When you think of the words "Corporate Wife," in the realm of charity, it might conjure up a different image than what's stereotypical, the image of a beautiful-on-the-inside woman, with her hair wrapped in a messy bun on her head with a colored hair-tie, in the latest workout clothes, in need of tomorrow's blow-out, wearing SPF 55 sunscreen, with a SmartWater in hand, her dog next to her, snoozing on the couch. She's smiling over the call she just received from her neighbor, who accidentally dialed her number, instead of the dog-runner. There are many opportunities for charity in the life of this Corporate Wife. Perhaps the real allure and mystique is that she is happy to be an active participant in charity that many people don't see—the charity that starts at home.

The Secret behind Being Charitable: *Being charitable helps HIM because it confirms that you are not all about you, but instead, you're about what you can do for others—starting with both your families.*

Pause and Consider

- If you aren't charitable, you aren't investing in the economy of your relationships. You're not giving back a portion of all that's been given to you. You're actually keeping other things from being added to you.

- Consider the possibility that:

  o Your husband wants charity to be important to YOU.

  o Your husband needs to see that you understand that everything you receive is not only for (and about) YOU.

  o Your husband loves when he sees charity that flows from the heart of YOU.

Kick-Ass Side Note—The Do & The Don't

DON'T DO THIS: Don't volunteer to the point where it continually interrupts your responsibilities to your husband, family, and priorities as a Corporate Wife.

DO THIS: Do have an "it comes back to you" attitude.

By being charitable, YOU set the tone by putting aside and giving a portion from all that's been given to YOU. It doesn't require much, but it does require something. Oftentimes, the most challenging gifts to give are the gifts that have the most rewards. There will be seasons in your life when you can open the door to be charitable. These seasons can make your husband proud and grateful for your giving heart. And that is how being charitable helps YOU.

* * *

Why are these 10 "secrets" or character traits important?

Without them, you won't be equipped to effectively handle the potential strife situations that will come your way as a Corporate Wife. These traits are your secret superpowers! These traits help build the foundation in the relationship you have with your husband. With these traits of character, you can make YOUR world a better place—so that you can make THE world a better place—and you can help others do it too, through your example. It IS possible to be the Kick-Ass Corporate Wife without friction and strife!

Remember my neighbor, who confessed to wanting my life for a week? Now that I've shared these ten "secrets" with you, perhaps your perception—as well as that of my neighbor's—conflicts with the idea that anyone would want my life. Marriage takes work. As you have read, the added element of being a Corporate Wife in marriage takes work too.

The Kick-Ass Corporate Wife isn't perfect. She just has some "secrets" in her arsenal. She's supportive, educated, courageous, creative, content, ambitious, good-natured, confident, kind, and charitable.

STEP 3 is where you ACCELERATE. The Corporate Wife has limitations . . . yet even still, she ACCELERATES in persevering with strength.

When she is ACCELERATING, she is STEPPING FORWARD with greater focus and intention to bring her VISION to fruition.

It may take a glass of wine or two, or biting her tongue on more occasions than not, but either way, she moves FORWARD and tries not to take herself, or life, so seriously. Perhaps that in itself is the resurrection . . .

Big Chapter Takeaways

- The Kick-Ass Corporate Wife is—

supportive	ambitious
educated	good-natured
courageous	confident
creative	kind
content	charitable

- STEP 3 is ACCELERATION. The Corporate Wife who ACCELERATES her STEPPING FORWARD gains momentum toward her VISION. It is through the process of taking each step with focus and eyes fixed straight ahead, moving forward at a sustainable yet momentous pace, that you rebuild your marriage into the abundant relationship you purposefully intend to create.

Up Next

In the next chapter I'm going to present a new way of viewing your role so that you can better master both the big picture of the Kick-Ass Corporate Wife Machine as well as its many moving parts. For it is how we understand each of our relationships in terms of the big picture that helps us interact in a kick-ass manner in the small ways to achieve a grand overall effect.

Third Action Plan

Ask yourself, "What's missing in me? What kind of person do I want to be? What can I do now to become more like that?"

Rate yourself on the "10 Secrets"— arrange them in order from one to ten, with one being the one you are most strong in and ten the least.

Let's take the three character traits you rated yourself as least strong in and the three you need the most work in. What you are going to do is strategically decide what, how, when, and where you'll engage with those three character traits over the next week. Assign one of these traits to a day in the next week and determine how you'll make the effort to engage with that trait on that particular day. This way, you deliberately start strengthening those weaker traits.

For example, say you've determined you most need to work with *educated*, *ambitious*, and *confident*. Here's how you could map it out to ensure you start engaging with these traits over the next week.

S	*Educated*—Listen to a TED Talk. Spend 10 minutes writing your thoughts about it in your journal.
M	*Ambitious*—Either sign up to take lessons to learn a language or to learn to play a musical instrument where you'll have to work one-on-one with an instructor outside the home.

T	*Confident*—Call a friend whom you haven't spoken with in a few months to catch up.
W	*Confident* and *Educated*—Take an intro class in a hands-on subject that's new to you, such as digital filmmaking, tai chi, ceramics, or sailing. Make sure it's a class where you must leave your home and participate with others of all ages.
Th	*Educated* and *Ambitious*—Go online to edX and browse the free, online university classes for 20 minutes. Sign up for a personal development course.
F	*Ambitious*—Spend 20 minutes exploring bathroom design on the Internet.
S	*Confident*—Invite one or two casual friends you like but don't know well to go out for coffee, a nature walk, or an art gallery walk with you.

I highly encourage you to continue deliberately scheduling these three traits into your daily life for many weeks beyond just this one!

5—Your Counterpart Role in Business

He's always asking, "Is that new? I've never seen that before."
It's like—why don't you mind your own business?
Go solve world hunger. Get out of my closet!
—Michelle Obama, First Lady of the United States

As we touched on in chapter 3, there's a lot going on behind the scenes with your responsibilities, your connections to your husband's business, your lifestyle, and the choices you make. So now we will address the role of the Corporate Wife as she works as the successful counterpart with her husband in their business-related activities. This is where the "Corporate" comes into play in the role of "Corporate Wife." It is your "business" role, even though you aren't necessarily clocking in at an office at 8 am.

Corporate Culture

Dressing the part of a Corporate Wife is just part of the equation, but it's an important one. We've already covered the importance of what's on the inside in terms of your traits of character. But there are also some "dos and don'ts" related to your exterior and what you put on display for others to see. Just as your husband's business has a corporate culture in terms of attire (his office may require he be dressed in a shirt and tie, or khakis and a polo shirt), you will need to follow suit with your attire to maintain a similar semblance of dress that complements his work culture when you participate in corporate-related activities.

Dress Code Compliance

I'm not implying that you have to start dressing *business casual* or wear a business suit and pumps around the house. What I am implying is that we *reframe* the picture of the Corporate Wife role in relation to the unspoken code of rules and comply with the lines in helping, and not hindering, business. There is an appropriate dress code that you need to follow, depending on the activity and the location.

As a Corporate Wife, you have a counterpart role to your husband, but it's not quite as demanding as other roles. The First Lady of the United States, for example, has had four successive primary themes since the early 1900s: as public woman, as political celebrity, as political activist, and as political interloper. Her position is not an elected one and, like yours and mine, carries no official duties. Nonetheless, First Ladies have held highly visible positions in US government. The role of the First Lady has evolved. She is, first and foremost, the hostess of the White House. She organizes and attends official ceremonies and functions of state either along with, or in place of, the President.

Some First Ladies have garnered attention for their dress and style. Jacqueline Kennedy, for instance, became a global fashion icon. Her style was copied by commercial manufacturers and imitated by many young women, and she was named to the International Best-Dressed List Hall of Fame in 1965. Michelle Obama has also received significant attention for her fashion choices: style writer Robin Givhan praised her in *The Daily Beast*, arguing that the First Lady's style has helped to enhance the public image of the office.

Similarly to First Ladies, the Corporate Wife's style can help enhance the public image of her position. When the Corporate Wife is traveling to other parts of the country, she needs to consider the location, its "clothing culture," the activities and functions she'll be engaging in there, and the weather and season. The accepted attire of trendy Los Angeles is quite different than that of the more conservative Washington, DC, or that of the opposite side of the world—in the climate of somewhere like Cape Town, South Africa. You have to do a little research and plan accordingly.

There's always a bit of the unknown, in terms of appropriate dress, when you are traveling with your husband and joining guests whom you've never met in another city. Even if you know the guests whom you will be with, you may not know for sure if you packed the appropriate clothing. This is where taking cues from various authorities can provide you with a sense of confidence.

Packing for the Unexpected

One particular business trip landed my husband and me in Miami Beach. I knew that I would need to step up my game in terms of what I would pack for our dinners in some upscale, contemporary restaurants. The weather was like summertime, so I would need to look the part and dress appropriately—keeping in mind brighter colors, shorter dresses, and, of course, designer handbags and high heels.

After getting my hair blown out, my makeup done, and joining our guests at the restaurant in a high-end hotel, I didn't plan for what could happen beyond my stellar suitcase-packing abilities: I started breaking out in a full-blown rash on my face! I had an allergic reaction to shellfish that left me looking like the character Will Smith played in the movie *Hitch*. Fortunately, my reaction wasn't so severe that I needed an EpiPen or to be rushed to the emergency room, but I was close.

The lesson: one thing you always want to be prepared for, no matter how many outfits you pack, is the plan for an unexpected emergency that will affect your appearance and your ability to associate with your husband's clients. (In other words, pack some liquid allergy medication in your travel bag in case you, or someone else, needs it!)

In another example, yet not as potentially life-threatening, my husband and I were having dinner with another couple in Las Vegas. My husband had not met this man's wife, but his perception was that she might resemble a twin sister to the actress, comedian, and model Sofia Vergara. Since we were in Las Vegas, and just about any attire goes in that town, I wore something that could be a little flashy, yet not too much, just in case she turned out to be different than what my husband expected. Sure enough, this couple was dressed comfortably, the wife wasn't flashy at all, and we had a wonderful dinner together.

What's my point? In situations where you don't know exactly how to dress, wear something that takes it up a notch to enhance your image, but makes you feel comfortable at the same time.

Pause and Consider

- Recall a time when you "got it right" in terms of packing, planning, and emerging in the perfect attire to a business-related event, weekend, or outing. Reflect on the considerations you took into account that resulted in your getting it right.

- Now recall a time when the opposite happened—when something about your appearance was just off. What did you fail to take into account that resulted in your getting it wrong? Often when we get it wrong, that's when we do the most learning. So what big lesson did you learn from this little misadventure?

Activities

Just as there's a corporate culture for your husband's business in terms of dress code, there is also a corporate culture in terms of activities. These can include corporate functions, sporting activities, annual parties, trade shows, galas, and dinners. You will need to know how to behave and participate accordingly.

Some situations go beyond merely dressing the part for activities as your husband's counterpart. The areas that overlap business and social activities can sometimes be a little tricky. They often require careful maneuvering and "big picture" thinking. It's like channeling your inner Princess Kate (Catherine—Duchess of Cambridge) to handle every delicate situation appropriately so that you'll reflect style and grace, while leaving a positive, lasting impression. Keep this in mind: *WWPKD?* as in **W**hat **W**ould **P**rincess **K**ate **D**o?

Things That Make You Go Hmmm

You might think you're safe because you're dressed in the right outfit, for a specific activity, but you still have to be careful and tread lightly when you delve into the culture mix of business and pleasure. Your outfit isn't going to protect you when you, unknowingly, find that you've jumped into shark-infested waters. You will experience moments during your active participation that run the gamut from awkward, to downright unfortunate in your role as a Corporate Wife.

An awkward experience happened to me once during a first-time encounter, mixing business and social time with two other couples. As we were conversing, while I was seated next to my husband, one of the Corporate Wives went out of her way to reach across me to secure her hand on my husband's forearm. In this position, she purred, "I *love* the way you think."

Lesson learned: your cute outfit doesn't protect you from the woman who oversteps the boundary—and your personal space—

to flirt with your husband . . . both in front of you and in front of her husband!

My husband and I are secure in our relationship. Yet this situation was not only awkward, it was a little weird. I chose not to react to it immediately, and thankfully, that was the first thing I got right. The second thing I did correctly was to later ask the other Corporate Wife who was with us, in confidence, if I saw the situation as she did. Was the woman a little tipsy? Or was I overreacting?

The outcome was that we both agreed that we viewed the situation the same (i.e., weird), but that it was something typical of this woman's outgoing behavior. I chose to view it as a minor offense I would simply overcome. Out of our mutual respect for this woman's husband, we agreed that although it was awkward, it was harmless. Even still, I made a mental note to decide if there would be future activities that would involve this wife.

If It Doesn't Fit, You Must (uh . . .) Quit

Some corporate couples participate in charity galas for a mix of business and pleasure. My husband and I have committed to attending one event per year, maximum. One year we attended a charity fashion show.

Several other Corporate Wives were participating with me as models in the charity fashion show. One of the wives—without asking me—lent my favorite pair of Manolo Blahnik pumps—which was the one pair of shoes I'd brought with me that coordinated perfectly with my pre-scheduled outfit—to another model with feet much larger than mine. When this wife saw my "Hey, wait a minute!" expression, she flung her hair around and declared with bravado, "Just send me the *receipt*, and I'll buy you another pair!"

Lesson learned: your perfectly fitting pair of designer shoes won't be protected from someone's use of your personal property . . . or someone else's big feet!

Sometimes you have to stop to look at the activities you're involved in and decide if you want to continue or not. I chose to respond to this situation by looking at how my support of these charity fashion shows served me and my husband. I was grateful for the opportunity to attend, help the friend in charge, and give to the community. I was grateful for the validation that my efforts to take good care of my health were paying off. But the time and effort involved in participating in the preparation for these lengthy shows, the hours spent commuting back and forth to attend these events, and the annoyances I experienced during them left me feeling drained and spent. Yes, some charities have uncharitable sides, so we must learn to be selective about where we put our time, energy, and resources.

Now when my husband and I attend the one annual charity event together, I no longer participate in what's going on behind the scenes. This works perfectly for both of us!

These two experiences resulted in boundary issues that, unfortunately, happen. What's your behavior going to be in those awkward moments where you look the part but find yourself swimming with the sharks? I'd like to respond as I *think* you would and agree that we'd like to give both of these women our two cents—or a big ole punch in the nose. But let's be honest— WWPKD? Princess Kate wouldn't do that.

What's my point? The Kick-Ass Corporate Wife shouldn't either. So, ask yourself the question, "What would *this* Kick-Ass Corporate Wife Do?" and then *do it*. Become more. Reflect your personal style in clothing and your personal grace in behavior to leave a lasting positive impression.

Removed from the A-List

Some situations can get unpredictably unfortunate. For example, my husband and I were having dinner out of town with another couple at one of our favorite restaurants. We were seated next to a foursome of two couples, who were deep in conversation. My Corporate Wife friend, seated next to me on the booth side of our table, whispered in my ear that she knew the woman seated at the table next to us. I could tell my friend's husband didn't know this woman from Adam, yet there was more to this story.

It was clear that my friend was not going to face the woman to say hello. Apparently, this woman had removed my friend from the guest list at a popular gala in town for "political" reasons, and something nasty happened. Lesson learned: your beautiful gala gown won't protect you from another's unpredictable and unfortunate behavior—but that doesn't mean that you should behave the same way in return.

When my friend shared this scenario with me, I realized we will all face unpredictably awkward, annoying, and unfortunate situations in which we still have to interact with, or will unknowingly encounter, challenging people connected to business and social activities. But when you crown yourself the Kick-Ass Corporate Wife, you have to consider the outcome of these encounters and how YOU want to handle them.

These stories are real-life situations that require us to NOT sweep our feelings under the rug or hide or make someone wrong; instead, they call us to take inventory. It's perfectly acceptable to acknowledge the pain and bewilderment involved in such situations. But we need to find a way to overcome these offenses, so we can be free to STEP FORWARD and not let them trip us up. We aim to be happy, peaceful, loving, merciful and forgiving people, and the way we do it is by making the choice to become more.

From Sideways to Grounded

I'm going to share with you my personal set of *20/20 Foresight Questions* that I ask myself to gain grounding when I detect a social situation going sideways.

Asking yourself these *20/20 Foresight Questions* should bring greater clarity to your outcome, i.e., the big picture.

- What is the best way to respond so that I can overcome the offense of this person's behavior?

- How can I "turn the other cheek?"

- Where do I balance my participation with the time and energy involved?

- [Later on, ask yourself] What would have caused the outcome of the situation to be different?

- [Later on, ask yourself] How can I confirm that I viewed the situation correctly?

In essence, once you recognize a situation is going sideways, and you pause and ask yourself the *20/20 Foresight Questions* (instead of reacting in haste), you can create the opportunity to respond with grace. This is how you experience growth, one step at a time, one scenario at a time. In the big picture, if a similar scenario happens again, you will do better next time. You can choose to not let someone's crossing of boundaries stunt or paralyze you, and leave you feeling angry or inferior. You can choose to become more.

Learning to behave with 20/20 foresight as the better person, counting to ten (or ten thousand), and taking the high road will almost always serve YOU. Realizing that these moments, too, shall pass, enables you to decide on the outcome YOU want. You can handle awkward, annoying, and unpredictable people and situations. If I can do it, you can too!

My point is this: become *more*. Become more of the person you want to be known for being.

Perhaps it means spending less time with certain people or opting out of certain events. Or maybe it means waiting and acknowledging the person and the situation later, privately, in a different way, when your feathers aren't ruffled. When you find yourself in a predicament that needs resolution, but you're not sure how to go about it, give the situation time and space. Give yourself permission to be selective.

Eventually you can decide whether supporting a particular person, or cause, is worth your time and energy. If you decide it is worth it, when you're ready, you can explain your feelings, without blame or making someone "wrong," and clear the air.

What will give YOU freedom? You get to choose the outcome. You can become more of who you want to be in every situation. You decide. This is a very freeing way to live for you, your husband, and everyone else whom you choose to surround yourself with.

Dos: Do take the time to reflect on your personal behavior. Beyond reflecting your personal style in clothing, emit your personal grace in behavior to leave a lasting, positive impression wherever you show up.

Don'ts: Don't react. Think big picture because we live in a small world.

STEP 4 is all about AUTHORITY. Seeking an AUTHORITY can help you get to the next step on your journey of becoming more. Seeking AUTHORITY leads you to reaffirm yourself so that you can get beyond any temporary obstacles and move into the greatness that is intended for you.

Resurrected examples of authority figures past (i.e., Grace Kelly, Jacqueline Onassis) and modern-day authorities (from Princess

Kate, to many of our First Ladies, to the examples of Kick-Ass Corporate Wives quoted in this book) help us understand that style and grace can permeate our strength. This is a key component for success in our roles. Like it or not, the truth is, we are constantly being watched and judged. But we can handle it. We can learn from the examples of these women when we get stuck in various predicaments so that we can move forward and grow in all of our interactions.

For it is how we understand each of our relationships in terms of the big picture that helps us interact in a kick-ass manner to achieve a grand overall effect.

Dos: Do make the effort to reflect excellence in your clothing and personal style by seeking AUTHORITY from a variety of sources. Comb the magazines for "must-have" pieces (such as a particular handbag and shoe) that make you look polished and right on-trend. Find a personal stylist in a virtual setting, at a department store, or seek assistance at a boutique that you love. (If the people who work at the boutique go out of their way to help you with suggestions and provide you with multiple sizes, colors, and styles, it's a tremendous help.) Study the style philosophies and tips of Lloyd Boston, Stacy London, or Tim Gunn. Download an app, such as "The Style App," to catalogue the items in your closet.

Do put the same effort into reflecting your positive style in behavior by channeling and resurrecting the examples of AUTHORITY figures in the public eye. Don't compare yourself to others—compare yourself to YOUR best self. Look to the potential of who YOU are capable of being: someone who is clothed in excellence in all you do.

Don'ts: Don't overdo it or wear something that makes you feel too uncomfortable. If you're going to be walking around a trade show, be aware that your feet are going to bark if you're not used to wearing stiletto heels all day. Don't be afraid to ask for guidance!

Don't behave with 20/20 hindsight. Don't play small when you get in a predicament. Choose, instead, to grow. Be the bigger, better person. Become more by growing forward.

Kick-Ass Side Note—The Do & The Don't

DON'T DO THIS: Don't over react and don't overdo it. Don't behave in a way that will make you uncomfortable in the future, and don't wear something that makes you feel uncomfortable in the present.

DO THIS: Do reflect the potential of who YOU are capable of being. Grow forward in your behavior and personal style. Do seek AUTHORITY from a variety of fashion sources and role models so that you can reflect excellence in the way you look and behave.

Big Chapter Takeaways

- Even though you aren't an employee of your husband's business, in order to support him and enhance his business relationships, there is an expected dress code for you.

- Remember that the dress code is particular to the place you are going and the activity you'll be engaging in there.

- In addition to how you look, how you act and react play major factors in your appearance. The key to acting and reacting with grace and style lies in the question: What Would a Kick-Ass Corporate Wife Do?

- Step 4 is AUTHORITY. Seeking AUTHORITY helps you move forward, all the while, fulfilling your role and responsibilities so that you can become more. Seeking AUTHORITY allows you to move forward with even greater determination, style, and grace. Seeking AUTHORITY allows you to reaffirm yourself, which in turn reinvigorates you on your journey of becoming more—of becoming a Kick-Ass Corporate Wife.

Up Next

We will take you from finding that perfect balance of fulfilling your role and your responsibilities as the counterpart role to your husband's business to the next step where you can make a helpful contribution to your husband's business, which in effect, is your shared livelihood. To give you a heads-up on what to expect: attentiveness is the name of the game!

6—Participation with Purpose

If you are successful, it is because somewhere, sometime, someone gave you a life or an idea that started you in the right direction.
—Melinda Gates, Businesswoman and Philanthropist

My husband shared his Gallup personality test results with me recently. This test is something used to evaluate specific employees in his business. He claims that it helps management to have a greater understanding of each person's strengths.

My husband's results were almost exhausting to read because he seemed like Superman! His only recommendation for improvement was that he should allow himself to experience a whisper of discontent now and then, and perhaps, do some yoga. Discontentment, like dissatisfaction, is a symptom of ambition. It means becoming more, but it also means that you have to be careful not to become a slave to your ambition and, instead, let it fuel your growth.

I've taken some other personality tests before (Meyers-Briggs, and my preferred test, Kolbe A Index) as I've already mentioned in chapter 4, and I believe I have a good understanding of my strengths and limitations. Instead of looking at his results with a competitive nature, I choose to look at his results in terms of how I can be an extension of them.

Your Husband's Impact

Most Corporate Wives are married to, more or less, in one way or another, a Superman of sorts. Men who make decisions. Big decisions. Decisions that affect the lives of others and their destinies, and decisions that affect the world. So what does that say about you?

To me, it says that you, directly or indirectly, affect those decisions too.

Warren Buffett has been quoted as saying about Melinda Gates, who is extremely protective of her family's privacy, that she helps her husband, Bill Gates, be a better decision-maker because she tends to see the whole-world picture. Credited by her husband for her desire to work full-time on foundation efforts, Melinda Gates helps drive a daunting list of initiatives, including expanding educational opportunities in the United States and improving health and reducing extreme poverty around the world (*Success Magazine*, "Women of Influence, by Erin Casey, April 14, 2009).

Your Impact

Similar to Melinda Gates, you are the behind-the-scenes Superpower Supporter of your Superman, not just his supportive appendage.

You, the Kick-Ass Corporate Wife, are comparable to the modern-day rocket fuel, the Bullet Proof® Coffee, that ignites your husband's ability to be strong, vibrant, and at his kick-ass best.

His Kryptonite

When my husband gets back from an intense time of business travel, he might be exhausted. Superman can only be super for so long without running out of gas. It might require that I let him wake up in the middle of the night to open his laptop when his schedule is off-kilter and he can't sleep. Or I might just go ahead and get up very quietly if he needs to sleep in longer. There are a lot of ways to fuel his fire, and sleep is a necessary component of many forms of fuel.

So what does it entail for you to be that fuel to his fire? That Superpower Supporter of your Superman? What are your responsibilities?

Pause and Consider

- Take a moment to articulate your husband's areas of limitation or need.

- Now consider both how you already support him and can enhance that support when he's in need.

Corporate Wife Confidential

This isn't a book about a set of rules. This isn't an Emily Post etiquette tome of 1922. But this is a resurrection in the context of the role of the Corporate Wife. There is a "Confidential Code of Ethics in Attentiveness."

Is attentiveness the same as obedience? I don't look at it that way. I see it more in the realm of social norms. There is a line you need to be attentive *not* to cross.

Attentiveness is a multifaceted realm. The significant elements of attentiveness that the Kick-Ass Corporate Wife must heed are these: attentiveness to appearance, attentiveness to communication, attentiveness to influence, and attentiveness to impact.

Here's an example of how "Ethics in Attentiveness" comes into play.

One morning, my husband reminded me that we had a corporate dinner party to attend that evening. It would be located in a casual environment, and I might be the only woman at the dinner party.

What this means to me in terms of attentiveness to my responsibilities:

- I am relieved of cooking dinner that night.

- I need to be ready to walk out the door by 5:45 pm.

- I need to show some enthusiasm and excitement concerning the possibility of whom I will meet.

This is all done so that when I arrive at the dinner, I show up excited and enthusiastic to be there and ready to be actively engaged.

What this means to me in terms of attentiveness to my appearance:

- It's a good reason to get my hair blown out that day. (Yay!)

- It's a good thing I got a manicure, pedicure, and my lash extensions touched up the previous day. (Whew!)

- I can compile a cute, casual outfit to wear that is appropriate for the occasion. (I'm prepared because I have an app for that!)

This is all done so that I can do my part, in terms of appearance, to look good for myself and for my husband.

This may seem like an arcane reference, in terms of attentiveness, but stick with me and hear me out. Trust me. Your appearance at these corporate dinners matters.

Attentiveness to Appearance

Where appearance plays out, in terms of attentiveness:

One of the men at this dinner was asking me questions about my background and our family. In the course of this conversation, he was, in a polite way, measuring me up. Let's face it—you have about a 3- to 4-second window to make a good impression. Like it or not, people are always judging. In the course of 5 minutes, he commented with appreciation, after his mental evaluation, that I "do a really good job of keeping myself up." Hey, it's a nice compliment. I'll take it!

When the Corporate Wife doesn't do her best to look the part, here's the painful truth: she probably doesn't get invited to the party. I'm not saying you have to look perfect, but I am saying that you want to be a positive extension of, and not an embarrassment to, your husband. You want to positively impact his business relationships, not diminish them—and a graceful, stylish appearance plays a part in this.

Putting your best foot forward not only makes you feel more comfortable with yourself, it makes others feel more comfortable with you because you exude a positive energy. This positive energy affects your ability to communicate effectively. And it positively affects your husband's business—thus, your shared livelihood.

Attentiveness to Communication: Your Purposeful Push

I may appear extroverted, but I am, by nature, an introvert. Many of the people whom you meet, whom you admire, are naturally shy. An estimated one-third to one-half of the population are introverts. Women, such as Eleanor Roosevelt, Christina Aguilera, and Emma Watson, have something in common with me. Men, such as Darren Hardy, Jeff Bezos, and Sir Richard Branson, do too. If these outliers of world change purposefully pushed themselves out of their shells, then you can, and need, to do it, too. If you engage people, they will be delighted, if not relieved, to have someone take the initiative.

Your Preparedness

What this means to me in terms of attentiveness to my communication skills:

- I need to ask my husband what to expect about the conversations that could come up in the course of the evening. Is there any topic to avoid? Is there anything that could cause me to stick my foot in my mouth?

- Go first. Smile first. Say hi first. Stick out your hand to meet someone first. Compliment someone first.

- I need to have my 30-second elevator pitch in my arsenal, in case I get asked some questions about myself, my family, or my personal interests.

- I need to be more willing to ask questions AND listen than to talk about myself. But it's also important to note that, in asking questions, no one wants to feel grilled. It needs to be a comfortable volleying back and forth.

- I need to be present, engage with people, and watch body language—mine and theirs.

- I need to be careful not to "trap" someone into conversation and allow everyone the ability to mingle.

- I need to be attentive to areas where I can help and not be too proud to extend a helping hand of service.

When the group of us was gathered for cocktails and appetizers, I noticed the body language of the crowd. One of the wives arrived with her husband, so aside from the two of us, the rest of the group was men. The men were, gradually, gathering in a circle discussing something related to business. It wasn't that the two of us were shut out, but one of the men had inadvertently stood in a place that caused this wife to be in the background.

Your Awareness

This is where I can be attentive and valuable, and make it a win/win for both of us, instead of having either of us feel left out. What inevitably happens is that one of the men in the conversation gets bored with the circle and joins ours. This is where the fun starts—especially if a glass of wine or two is involved—because the crowd loosens up a bit and real conversation can begin and lead to an enjoyable evening, where everyone is comfortable and a positive outcome is on the way.

An easy way to guide conversation and keep someone talking about themselves is through a simple model I learned from speaker, trainer, and success coach Dani Johnson in her book *First Steps to Wealth*. The model uses the acronym **F.O.R.M**:

1 **F**amily

2 **O**ccupation

3 **R**ecreation

4 **M**essage

Go first. Help ease someone else's shyness, even if it's your own. Be willing to win first. Compliment first. (What interesting shoes you have!)

When the opportunity arises during a lull in a natural conversation, start asking some easy questions. Start by asking people about their **f**amily (tell me about you—where are you from? Do you like where you live? Are you married/single? Do you have kids?). Then ask about their **o**ccupation (do you work outside the home? What do you do for a living? How did you get started? How long have you been doing it?) and about **r**ecreation (what do you do for fun? Do you participate in any sports? Have you been doing it for a long time?). It is a way to find out what people are interested in and to show interest in them. Get people talking about those three things.

Your Interest

One of the best things you can do, as a Corporate Wife, is be interested in other people regardless of how it benefits you. This is how you honor people, impact their lives for the better, and sow good seeds. After the focus is put on them with those three things—family, occupation, and recreation—then the message (related to business) is ready to be discussed . . . and usually that happens over the dinner table.

 Pause and Consider

- Review my list of what's necessary to be prepared to be an excellent communicator.

- From this list, decide which elements you are great at and which elements you can improve on.

- Check your calendar to determine the date of the next business dinner. Choose one of those elements that you need to focus on—and write it in as your goal for that dinner. Another option here is to have the goal to employ the "family, occupation, and recreation" method of engaging someone in conversation.

- After the dinner, reflect on how you improved in that goal area.

Attentiveness to Influence

What this means to me in terms of attentiveness to table manners:

- Be aware of how much you put on your plate (if food is passed) so that everyone gets their portion and you don't look like you're starved.

- Be aware of how much you drink if alcohol is involved so that you maintain your composure and ability to communicate effectively.

- Be aware of how much you say so that you don't say too much, come off as someone who doesn't shut up, come off as someone who is boastful, or come off as someone who is judgmental and says something rude about what the other person puts on their plate. Bring something positive and helpful to the table.

- Be aware that your potential current food kick (e.g., gluten-free, vegan, raw, or non-GMOs) is likely uninteresting, distracting, or even annoying to others at the table, so keep quiet about it—and do not talk about how the food on anyone's plate measures up to your current obsession.

- Be aware of something caught in your teeth, and sneak away to get rid of it!

- Be aware of how you make a graceful and gracious exit.

Pause and Consider

- As you did in the previous *Pause and Consider*, you are going to do it again—only in terms of table manners. From the "Attentiveness to Influence" list, decide which elements you are great at and which elements you need to improve on.

- Choose one of those elements that you need to focus on—and write it in your calendar as your goal for the next business dinner.

- After the dinner, reflect on how you improved in that goal area of table manners.

Attentiveness to Impact

You want to go into this situation and leave this situation knowing that you did your part to ensure that the people you meet view you in a positive light and look forward to your next meeting. Your attentiveness at the dinner has a great impact on your husband's business.

The world is a small place. You'd be surprised how many times we meet people in business, only to find that we are somehow connected, in some "how crazy is that?!" way. It happens all the time.

Dos: Do your best to make a great first and final impression. When you fulfill your responsibilities and fuel them with your secret, superpower ammunition of supreme attentiveness, you look, act, and behave the part of the Kick-Ass Corporate Wife.

Don'ts: Don't forget that the world is a small place. Your actions go with you, whether you like it or not, wherever you go—or don't go.

This is where the previous four steps that you've taken culminate into the final step of greatest impact: *contribution*. STEP 5 is CONTRIBUTION. You, being who you uniquely are, with your superpower traits of character, are making a CONTRIBUTION to yourself, to your husband's business, and to others.

If we go back to the beginning in STEP 1, your VISION was to be other-centered on your husband in your marriage. In STEP 2, you took a STEP FORWARD toward that VISION. In

STEP 3, you ACCELERATED the steps and the "10 Secrets" toward your VISION with momentum. In STEP 4, you sought help from various AUTHORITIES, when you got stuck, with that VISION in mind. Finally, you arrive at STEP 5, making a CONTRIBUTION in ways beyond your VISION for your marriage—your VISION transcended into his business and to your personal impact and potential.

Kick-Ass Side Note—The Do & The Don't

DON'T DO THIS: Don't ignore your secret superpowers of contribution and impact.

DO THIS: Do your best to make a great first and final impression by being attentive to your appearance, your communication, your table manners and your overall impact.

Big Chapter Takeaways

- In supporting your husband and enhancing his business relationships, your attentiveness is crucial.

- Your attentiveness to your appearance, your communication, and your table manners plays a great role in your impact, positive or negative, on a business event. Your attentiveness is your secret superpower!

- The highly attentive Kick-Ass Corporate Wife makes a great first and final impression.

- STEP 5 is CONTRIBUTION. The Corporate Wife, who CONTRIBUTES to her corporate marriage and business, connects all of the dots from the starting point of VISION. She chips away at herself, her marriage, and the foundation she has established in her marriage to enhance the business relationships associated with her marriage. It is through CONTRIBUTION—the giving of yourself and the sowing of the seeds–that you receive more than you could ask, think, dream or imagine. You become the Kick-Ass Corporate Wife. It is the fifth and final step.

Up Next

In closing this book in the next chapter, we will revisit the book's whole purpose—establishing a firm foundation on which you, your husband, and your marriage can flourish. I'm going to share with you some details about one particular rock-solid marriage that so many naysayers initially doubted. How wrong they were!

7—Final Thoughts

A successful marriage starts with the foundation of your relationship.
—Kathryn Ann Srb, devoted Wife, Mother, Mother-in-law,
Grandmother, Aunt, and Friend

My goal in writing this book, and its accompanying guide, is to put a simple structure in place to help you build a foundation for the relationship you have with your husband. However, I hope you have taken away much more from this book than just this goal, your "relationship," or your "role."

I hope that, after successful application of the principles and action plans of this book, you feel ready to create a strategy for your own vision for your life. This isn't my book, about my vision, it's YOURS!

I also hope that after getting to know me through these words, you believe that I'm more to you than just a Corporate Wife's good juju, or a good Samaritan. I hope you see me more as your real Encouragement Helmswoman, steering you in a positive direction. On this journey, I hope you've discovered that I've got your back, I've got you covered, and if it works out that our interests are aligned, then there's no stopping us!

The big idea at the heart of this book is threefold:

1   There is more.

2   Become more.

3   YOU are more!

In this book, where we start at the foundation level of a woman, a woman in marriage, a woman in a role as a wife to a busy corporate guy, there is more than this "title" of Corporate Wife. There is more for you, and for others, to realize and discover about you.

To succeed in finding more purpose, fulfillment, freedom, joy, and all the things that help you live out your highest potential, all you have to do is become more.

To become more, you start by building your marital foundation with those 5 steps that lead you to your version of success in this role. I've provided you with my top 10 "secrets" to success although many character traits could be expanded on and even added to the list. These traits are a tool for measure—a plumb line—similar to what masons use to make sure they lay up a brick wall straight and true.

By incorporating excellence into yourself, you expand the better, best, most excellent traits of who you already are. You ARE more than a Corporate Wife—you ARE a Kick-Ass Corporate Wife.

When you start from a place of nothing much at all, when you're bored, frustrated, and feeling like an appendage, you have to be laser-focused on the vision of where you'd rather be in this role— succeeding at it! The more you need to succeed, the more likely that you will. The more emotional and personal investment in your marriage—the more you'll get back, and become, in return.

There is great power in being a Corporate Wife—when you have a fire inside, a willingness to do whatever it takes to succeed in your life.

When your plumb line is in alignment with your through line— that golden thread that weaves through your marriage—that's when all the dots get connected to living your truest and biggest life. That's where you need to be, in whatever way you choose to be. That's when you start inspiring others and transforming the lives of those around you. That's when those who are watching you, who see something beautiful in you, start to see something beautiful in themselves, and the world becomes a better place . . . because you're in it!

Your marital foundation is built, you've crossed this particular finish line, and now it creates a new starting point on your journey. It's where you begin again, equipped and established and ready to take that next step toward a brand-new vision. I hope that this expands your journey of continually finding the places where your passions, talents and interests all connect so that you can sustain yourself while doing all the things you truly love.

I hope that the message of this book is relevant in your life at every stage you find yourself in, as you continually evolve and grow as a person.

* * *

This year marks the 65th wedding anniversary of my parents.

My dad will be the first person to tell you that he hit the jackpot that day he eloped with my mother when she was only 19 and he was 22. They didn't even tell anyone that they were married . . . for 3 months! Times were different back then, and they assumed their decision wouldn't be supported by their parents. So, they simply went back to their respective houses and kept their marriage a secret. *Can you imagine that? I can't either!*

Their marriage secret was finally revealed when tax time neared. Unfortunately, their assumption that they would get a negative reaction from both sides of parents turned out to be correct. Based on parental opinion, the odds against them were great that their marriage wouldn't last. Yet, I'm here to tell you that my parents, who secretly eloped to Iowa as a young couple, defied the odds.

The longevity of their marriage says something about their success as a counterbalanced team:

My 6'4" father, the son of a physician and his supportive wife, is known for his friendly smile and kind demeanor. He's the type of person who would be the first to pull over to help you if he saw that your car was stopped alongside the road. He always "had his nose in the job" as he did his part to support his family of five kids.

My 5'4" mother, the daughter of an attorney and his supportive wife, stayed home to raise my siblings and me. She has the patience of a saint, a quiet superpower strength, a content attitude, and tremendous strategizing and systemizing abilities. She's the kind of mother you hear humming a hymn while she washes dishes in the kitchen, as the aroma of chocolate-chip, oatmeal cookies baking in the oven fills the air. She makes any house feel like a home. She is always doing something behind the scenes. She is never the center of attention.

Between the two of them, I'll never know how they kept everything together. They have had their share of trials and tribulations. How they managed all the details behind the scenes is something I wasn't privy to while I was growing up. They aren't perfect people, but they are excellent examples of their commitment to each other. They do what they *choose* to do. They focus on their family—and they do it out of *love*.

Because of their example, as a loving couple, as loving parents, and because of my mother's example as a devoted wife—doing what she chose to do and doing it out of love—I learned the most important secret: I learned to see the sky instead of the ceiling.

Today, I am resurrecting the traditional role in marriage. Now, I am doing what I choose to do—sharing my belief—and I'm doing it out of love.

I always believed that one day—*finally!*—my mother would get the opportunity to be the center of attention. She deserves the opportunity to shine, and I hope that the evidence of her light has been revealed through the title and the pages of this book.

My mother is my example of a woman who chose to become more by fulfilling her God-given destiny. She connected the dots in being herself first and by doing what resonated with her energy and passion. In doing what came naturally to her, she's found happiness. My mother's unique gift is making others be *her* center of attention. She helps others rise higher by becoming the miracle other people need—whether it's her voice, her hands, her arms to hug, her ears to listen—she is the answer to someone's prayer and that sign of encouragement.

She started helping others within the foundation of her marital relationship, and let it overflow into every life she touches. I believe in her. I believe she has something of value to share with everyone she comes into contact with. I believe what she shares is important.

Like her, I believe you do, too.

You're amazing! You're going to do great things.

There is more . . .

Become more . . .

YOU are more!

You've got what it takes to be a Kick-Ass Corporate Wife.

Starting now!

Additional Resources

Be sure to access these implementation tools as my gift to you:

Kick-Ass Corporate Wife® **Encouragement Guide** gives ideas, strategies, and tools you can use right now to start enhancing the foundation of your marriage. This is a helpful resource to use for personal reflection or when facilitating a book club.

Kick-Ass Corporate Wife® **Resources Guide** offers my favorite go-to solutions to save you time, money, and headaches.

www.SusanBurlingame.com/Book1

This book is whole and complete in and of itself, but if you want to take the next step to go farther with the *Kick-Ass Corporate Wife* series, stay tuned for Book 2.

For a complete and continually updated version of additional resources, please visit the resource page of my website at www.SusanBurlingame.com

Acknowledgments

I extend my appreciation and thanks to everyone who has made this book possible . . .

To God who is for me and is good all the time . . .

To the editing wizardry of Nancy Pile, who so eloquently captured the essence of my message and encouraged me to pull out the stories and references of my responsibilities and give my process order and coherence . . .

To the web design mastery of Kevin Gillotti of SCHEMA Internet Strategies Consulting™, whose expertise and boundless energy balances the follow-through of my ideas with creative implementation into my platform . . .

To the creative genius of The Draw Shop team, whose collective inspiration helped me communicate my story through a killer script, beautiful illustrations, and a unique whiteboard animation video . . .

To the design prowess of Alex Espinosa of The 750 Shop, whose competence and judgment refined my brand, content marketing, and product development.. . .

To the audio expertise of Dan Perreault, whose technical skills and audio-recording mastery delivered the best version of my authentic voice . . .

To the brilliant personal development experts I have worked with and learned from over the past two decades—all of the mentors, colleagues, and extraordinary achievers I have had the chance to glean new insights, ideas, and wisdom from . . .

To each and every one of my family members and friends who have partnered with me offering their relentless support, loving wisdom, and encouragement . . .

And finally, and most importantly, to my handsome and wonderful husband, Kevin, who (along with our dog, Sailor) is living proof that every good and perfect gift comes from God. I love you with all my heart.

About the Author

Susan Burlingame is the content creator for the blog "Healthy Stylish Life® for the Corporate Wife," and with it, challenges the highly functioning, overcommitted Corporate Wife to resurrect traditional marriage by creating purpose and fulfillment within the matrimonial role. Susan is the author of the upcoming second and third installment series to go with this book, as well as the creator of an interview-based podcast, Kick-Ass Corporate Wife. Her goal is for today's woman to follow her example and sustain her allure, find purpose, and fulfill her God-given destiny—all while kicking-ass in the marriage of her dreams. Susan is a graduate of Arizona State University and lives with her husband and their dog, Sailor, in Southern California.

Endnotes

Chapter One

1 Cindy Crawford. http://www.cindy.com
Quote source unknown.

2 Cindy Crawford and Rande Gerber:
"Tough Decisions Lifeclass," *Huffington Post*, April 8,
2014. (Retrieved October 1, 2016). The Gerber Group,
http://gerberbars.com/about (Retrieved October 1, 2016).

Chapter Two

3 The Real Housewives of Orange County.
http://www.bravotv.com/the-real-housewives-of-orange-
county (Retrieved October 1, 2016).

4 Sara Blakely. http://www.spanx.com
Darren Hardy, *SUCCESS Magazine*, January 2016,
SUCCESS.com, March 2016 Audio CD. (Retrieved
January 2016). Interview on *SUCCESS Talks Collectio*n,
YouTube. (Retrieved October 4, 2016).

5 Sara Blakely and Jesse Itzler:
"How I Built It: Marquis Jet," *Wall Street Journal*,
October 27, 2010 (Retrieved October 1, 2016).

Chapter Three

6 Barbara Corcoran. http://www.barbaracorcoran.com
"Barbara Corcoran interview on the realities of
entrepreneurial success," SUCCESS.com, March 2016,
Audio CD. (Retrieved March, 2016).

7   Barbara Corcoran and Bill Higgins:
    "The Most Henpecked Man In Manhattan," *New York Post*, May 12, 1999. (Retrieved October 4, 2016).

Chapter Four

8   Mary Kay Ash. https://www.marykay.com
    Quote source unknown.

9   Mary Kay Ash and Ben Rogers, Wikipedia®
    https://en.wikipedia.org/wiki/Mary_Kay_Ash (Retrieved August 31, 2016).

10 Mary Kay Ash and George Hallenbeck, and Richard Hallenbeck
    http://www.thefamouspeople.com/profiles/mary-kay-ash-251.php (Retrieved October 4, 2016).

11 Darren Hardy. http://darrenhardy.com
    SUCCESS Magazine http://www.success.com

12 Holy Bible, *New International Version, Proverbs* (Colorado Springs, Colo.: Biblica, 2011-2016), vs. 13:20 http://www.biblica.com

13 Tony Robbins. https://www.tonyrobbins.com
    Quote source unknown.

14 Virginia Woolf, A Room of One's Own, October 24, 1929. Virginia Woolf Seminar. University of Alabama, Huntsville. January 20, 1998. P.1. Archived from the original on December 24, 2012. (Retrieved December 24, 2012).

15 Williams Sonoma *Essentials of Healthful Cooking Cookbook*, (San Francisco, CA Weldon Owen, Inc. and Williams-Sonoma, Inc., 2008), 122.

16 Joe Polish. http://www.joepolish.com

Chapter Five

17 Michelle Obama, *New York Times*, "Mrs. Obama Speaks Out About Her Household." March 20, 2009 (Retrieved October 1, 2016).

18 Carl Sferrazza Anthony, "The Role of the First Lady", America.gov. (September 26, 2008). (Retrieved May 4, 2009).

19 Lisa M. Burns, *First Ladies and the Fourth Estate: Press Framing of Presidential Wives*. Dekalb, IL: Northern Illinois University Press, 2008. (Retrieved October 1, 2016).

20 Robin Givhan, (2012). "First Lady Fashion Fatigue". *The Daily Beast*. (Retrieved October 1, 2016).

21 VF Staff (1965). "World's Best Dressed Women". The International Hall of Fame: Women. *Vanity Fair*. (Retrieved February 15, 2012).

22 Bettina Zilkha, (2004). *Ultimate Style: The Best of the Best Dressed List*. New York, NY: Assouline. Pp. 64-49, 90. ISBN 2-84323-513-8. (Retrieved October 1, 2016).

23 2005 Sony Pictures Romance Comedy about Dating coach, Alex "Hitch" Hitchens, (Will Smith).

24 Princess Kate (Catherine Duchess of Cambridge), http://www.dukeandduchessofcambridge.org

25 Lloyd Boston. http://www.lloydboston.com
Stacy London. website unknown
Tim Gunn. website unknown
The Stylebook App. http://www.stylebookapp.com

Chapter Six

26 Melinda Gates, Valedictory speech, Ursuline Academy, 1982

27 Gallup Test, https://www.gallupstrengthscenter.com

28 Meyers-Briggs, MBTI, http://www.myersbriggs.org/my-mbti-personality-type/mbti-basics/

29 Kolbe-A Index, http://www.kolbe.com

30 Warren Buffett, *Success Magazine*, "Women of Influence" http://www.success.com/article/women-of-influence by Erin Casey, April 14, 2009 (Retrieved October 1, 2016).

31 Emily Post, *Etiquette in Society, in Business, in Politics, and at Home* (New York, Funk & Wagnalls, 1922, New York, Bartleby.com.,1999). (Retrieved October 1, 2016).

32 Eleanor Roosevelt, Christina Aguilera, Emma Watson, Darren Hardy, Jeff Bezos, Sir Richard Branson, http://www.darrenhardy.com/about/ (Retrieved October 1, 2016).

33 Dani Johnson, *First Steps To Wealth*, (Call To Freedom Int'l., 2011).

Chapter Seven

34 Kathryn Ann Srb, in-person conversation with author, February 28, 2016.